LEARNING
ABOUT
GOD

ALSO BY NORMAN KOTKER

LEARNING ABOUT GOD

NORMAN KOTKER

A DONALD HUTTER BOOK

HENRY HOLT AND COMPANY
New York

Published by Henry Holt and Company, Inc., 115 West 18th Street,
New York, New York 10011.
Distributed in Canada by Fitzhenry & Whiteside Limited,
195 Allstate Parkway, Markham, Ontario L3R 4T8.

Kotker, Norman.
Learning about God.
"A Donald Hutter book."
I. Title.
PS3561.0844L44   1988   813'.54   88-9492
ISBN 0-8050-0726-1

First Edition

Designed by M 'N O Production Services Inc.
Printed in the United States of America
1 3 5 7 9 10 8 6 4 2

Portions of this book appeared in *The Paris Review*.

The author wishes to thank The National Endowment for the Arts and the
Massachusetts Artists Foundation for grants which assisted in the comple-
tion of this book.

ISBN 0-8050-0726-1

In memory of the millions

In memory of the millions

... and in the dread hour before his death he spoke to Jacob and to the others who were by, in high and awe-inspiring tones, very darkly and oracularly, of "himself" as the rescued sacrifice, and of the blood of the ram, which was to be thought of as his own blood. ... Yes, just before the end he essayed with remarkable success to bleat like a sheep and his bloodless face took on an astounding likeness to the countenance of that animal—or rather, they were conscious all at once that the likeness had always been there.

—Thomas Mann, *The Tales of Jacob*

I

There are thousands of stories: Moses and the dead angels, Hitler and the birdcage, Theodor Herzl's trip to the moon. Only I know these stories. Only I tell them. This is the story of Chaim Fogel, the concentration camp survivor.

EVERY OCTOBER, in the season when the tree leaves are turning on earth and in heaven the leaves of the Book of Life are turning too, Fogel went to the Bergen-Belsen Survivors' Banquet at the Plaza or the Pierre. Naturally he preferred the Plaza, because of the hors d'oeuvres: avocado appetizers, little cubes with fresh-ground pepper on them and an outstanding Italian dressing. What did he care if the survivors crowded around the hors d'oeuvre table, a mob pushing furiously against each other to reach for a serving of smoked salmon with capers or pâté en croûte, just the way they had pushed in the camp trying to get a spoonful of potato peel soup. It didn't shame him. The irony wasn't lost on him. It pleased him to see the people milling around, their mouths continually moving; either they were talking or they were chewing. He liked to look at the women, at their dresses— low-cut, high-cut, tight, loose, purple, glassy-green, yellow, various reds; chiffons, prints, red-white-and-blue. He liked

1

the rooms the banquet was held in: mirrors on the wall, cherubs on the ceiling, frescoes, gilt, rococo mantelpieces, baroque chandeliers. He liked to look at the number of things in the room, what God had made: Jews, waiters, chairs, tables, chandeliers, salmons, glasses, ice cubes with their short glittering lives, bottles of liquor, matchbooks, matches, cigarettes, cigarette ashes. It was as if each hair on his head was numbered and accounted for. It satisfied him immensely.

But one summer day as he rode in from White Plains on the morning train, he turned to his friend Broitman sitting next to him, also a survivor, and said, "This year I won't go."

"Why not?" Broitman was indignant. "Why not? You have to go."

"To come into the city." A whimper. Fogel was a small-boned man, stunted. He would never look suburban. "A late night. To find a parking space. So much traffic, even on weekends." Although Fogel's wife, Lillian, had already purchased her outfit, a new dress, Bloomingdale's, White Plains, $130.

"What are you talking about?" Broitman golfed. He had an American suntan. A coat manufacturer, he had in certain years hired a car with a driver just for the evening to take him to the Plaza or the Pierre. "Don't be stupid. You shouldn't miss it. This year," he leaned closer to Fogel, heavily, "they're going to have a cake with a naked tootsie jumping out of it."

Jokes. Jokes. The Bergen-Belsen Banquet always gave rise to jokes.

Why? Because who, even among those who attended it, could ever believe that the survivors actually held a banquet? Though there was a report of it every year, very solemn, on one of the back pages of *The New York Times*. A sociologist had done a study: When readers saw the news item, they giggled. Unbelievable! Also disgusting. Vulgar. Blasphemous.

So what? No one had believed that the camps had existed either.

A joke. There were these two survivors who encountered each other at the banquet after twenty years; in the camp they had been reduced (ha-ha!) to cannibalism. They met at the hors d'oeuvre table. "You've gained a lot of weight," said A. "It's my job," said B. "I'm a tester."

"What do you test?"

"Cookbooks."

"Wonderful! A far cry from the old days."

"Not so much. My next book is: 'What to Cook When There's Nothing to Eat in the House.' "

Then there was the song Fogel's children had made up. Once he had heard them. He was sorry he had to shout to make them stop. Little Americans— What did they know about All-gones, about Bone-sacks, about No-faces? A cowboy song. "We're headin' for the last roundup. Git along, git along. Headin' for Bergen-Belsen. A-singin' a song." He and his wife, not a survivor, American-born, had been getting dressed to go out. The children were eight, ten, clever, they meant no harm. That's what children are for—they make fun.

"I'm not going," said Fogel. "I'm through. This year finished. All over. Kaput. That's it. Thumbs down."

"You'll change your mind," Broitman said as the train slid to a stop somewhere in the South Bronx.

An empty view: ruined tenements, deserted lots covered with smashed bricks, here and there a wall half knocked over. Desolation. Fogel was sorry he had a window seat. How long would they have to wait there? Would the air-conditioning go off? They'd suffocate.

"Never! Never! I'm through. I'm finished. I said it."

A personal statement. The revolt of the individual. Fine! Lovely! But would he show up there? "I'm through, I'm

3

through, I'm through," he said to his wife a few weeks later, after the invitation had come in the mail. "I'm through."

"What do you mean you're through? How can you be through?" She picked up the mail from the kitchen counter where the mail was kept and handed it to him aggressively. "This year the Plaza. What's better?"

"I always liked the Plaza," Fogel admitted. Without reading it, he firmly put the invitation back on the kitchen counter. Recently he had been very busy, working very hard; he was preparing his new course, NYU downtown. Almost no one took his "The Enlightenment" anymore. He had refused to change the name of the course to "The Dawn of the Revolution." Now even his "Introduction to Modern Europe" was losing enrollment. He was afraid they would drop him. What did tenure mean these days? "The Person in History" was what he was working up, or "The Person, Past and Present." Sometimes he thought it might be safest just to call it "The Person."

Was that why their sex life was deteriorating? Because he was so worried?

His son Steven was doing graduate work in California—in "Cool Media." Marlene, his daughter, was at Boston University getting an M.A. in "The Urban Experience."

With a contemptuous look at his wife, he went out into the yard to coil the garden hose. "Forget it," he said as he opened the kitchen door to walk out. "I'm through going. I'm through. Don't waste a postage stamp. Eight cents. Put the money in the bank, it will come in handy for your old age." He turned around and held his right hand out stiffly. "See! Finished. Rigor mortis." He let the screen door slam loudly behind him.

But it was apparent: The next day she would RSVP: Will attend, Mr. and Mrs. Chaim Fogel. Number of persons in

4

party: 2. And would enclose a check for $37.50. The price had gone up. But it didn't pay for a meal like that, not to mention drinks. The extra was paid for by a philanthropist, also a survivor.

So THEY WENT. "Aha, Fogel. I knew you would show up," Broitman said. "Abe Broitman is never wrong?"

Fogel was nibbling a frank in a blanket. He felt a little better. "The Person, Past and Present" it was; he had already seen the galley proofs of the next catalog. "The Person, Past and Present, Professor Fogel," it said. His wife was wearing a dress made out of silver material, but in good taste. With it she wore silver shoes. A nice color, it might indicate something favorable about his professional future. Some women were wearing dresses made out of gold. Businessmen's wives. When they moved, gold moved. He looked around to see if there were any other academics in the crowd. Unfortunately, the only ones he recognized were merely in Yiddish Studies.

His own appearance also was acceptable. He was wearing a dark blue suit, one hundred percent wool. His necktie was Italian silk, weighted, blue and silver. He could feel it snug around his neck. He could feel his black leather belt around his waist, his shining black shoes protecting his feet. The cattle, the silkworms, the sheep, they were dead. He was alive, drawing breath.

Occasionally people broke down at these affairs, at least one each year. Not just tears, men groaning, holding their foreheads with one hand, rocking from side to side; not just overdrinking, too much avocado, the fatty part of the duck and then after an hour of dancing horas or cha-chas, vomiting—if they were lucky, in the men's room, if not, as once happened, on the dance floor; not just that, but real break-

5

downs. One time a woman, weeping, shrieking, had to be dragged from the room. One time one of the organizers of the affair, a big contributor, a man sitting at the head table on the double dais, was slapped by another survivor, a woman. One time two men started fighting, fists, in the middle of the floor. Fogel didn't think he would break down. Now—it was time—he would treat the whole thing lightly. No, not lightly certainly, but in perspective: The Jews weren't the only people who had suffered. Look at all the people who had been tortured by their own parents; he knew of some cases. He had one colleague at NYU whose mother had made her eat dog food when she was a child; he knew someone else whose father and mother had both called him nothing but "Stinks"—even after he had grown up. He knew a man who worked for his father, in plastics, a big factory; all he did for twenty years was sweep the floor. "Schmuck, that's all you can do!" the father said. He knew addicts. He knew lesbians. These people also were lucky if they got out of it alive. Did they hold banquets?

His wife was not in sight anymore. He pushed through the crowd to look for her. Mostly survivors or survivors' mates, not many others. All people past middle age, tired, suspicious-looking. But his wife couldn't be seen, not even her reflection in the gilt-framed mirrors on the wall. By the time he found her, they would be reading the necrology already; they would be announcing the prize for the best concentration-camp book of the year; or even worse, reading excerpts from it, lights dimmed, no noise but the subdued voice of the reader and the tiptoeing of the black waiters bringing in the bombe glacé and after-dinner mints.

He found her at table number sixteen, talking to Broitman's wife, also an American.

"Is it fancy enough for you?" Broitman's wife asked. "It's fancy enough for me."

This year each table had as a floral centerpiece an Israeli flag, blue and white, made of carnations. On the wall above the head table was another floral arrangement: the words "BERGEN-BELSEN" in red roses on a ground of white carnations and beneath it, in Hebrew and English, the word "REMEMBER."

Fogel's wife approved. "It must have cost a fortune." Shy before her marriage, a published poet in the Hunter College literary magazine, she had rarely ventured to inspect the tattooed numbers on his arm; they made her too uneasy. For a time after they had met, one year, two years, they had discussed the camps obsessively—on dates, in bed, walking on Fordham Road, everywhere. She had held his head in her arms and he cried. Sometimes it was the other way around. She cried: Man's Inhumanity to Man—who could bear it!

He could bear it. He had borne it. "It's beautiful," he said to Mrs. Broitman. "How do they get the flowers blue? Do they grow that way? A variation?" He sat down beside his wife on the side away from the Broitmans. He didn't know who would be sitting next to him. They hadn't arranged a table. Whoever would come would sit there, catch as catch can. He knew idioms.

The music stopped for a moment, a gasp, then it transformed itself into a flourish. The urgent voice of the MC came charging over it. "This is it. Dinner is served. Ladies and gentlemen, please go to your tables. No lagging."

The crowd formed into little battalions. So many of them were plump. They settled obediently into their gold-backed, plush-upholstered chairs. "God, I'm starving," Fogel's wife said.

He patted her arm. He himself was not hungry at all.

7

The first course was fresh-fruit cup with sherbet, nothing fancy. But as Broitman's wife pointed out, at the Plaza fresh-fruit cup means fresh, and not all citrus fruits either.

"Mine has a piece of honeydew melon in it," Broitman said. He exhaled contentedly. "But it's too bad the sherbet is lime, not orange."

"I prefer lime," Lillian said, "it's more unusual."

The next course was puree mongole. Fogel took a spoonful. Then he stopped eating. He put his spoon down. He could feel the metallic taste of the spoon on the side of his tongue.

"What's the matter? Why aren't you eating it?" Lillian sounded relaxed, but she sat stiffly with her bosom close to the table because she was afraid of spilling on her new silver dress.

"I don't want to stuff myself." Fogel suffered from chest pains, heartburn. Cucumbers, mushrooms, melon—all these brought him grief. Tonight he was afraid it would happen again. Sometimes he felt it was bad enough to kill him.

"Don't you like it? I love it." Lillian was an enthusiast of international cooking. She made shrimp curries with shredded coconut; she made boeuf bourguignon, lasagna. She owned the *United Nations Cookbook*. The proceeds went toward international peace. "It's delicious," she said happily. "I wouldn't dare make it at home."

"Let someone in the kitchen eat it. Give it to the waiters. Let them put it in a dog bag for you, you'll take it home."

Quenelles was the next course. They were served with wine. Fogel drank the wine and took a little taste of the fish. Around the table the topic of conversation was this: It looks like gefilte fish, it tastes like gefilte fish, though with less flavor, but it isn't gefilte fish. "Quenelles," Lillian said, drawing out the word to the full, leaving the final *e* dangling. She had once made them, though they hadn't come out so light. Then Fogel had eaten several servings. This time he wasn't eating at all. "How much did you drink?" she whispered.

"Only one."

"I hate to see it go to waste." As soon as she finished her fish, she deftly transferred plates, with a little wink at Mrs. Broitman, and ate Fogel's serving too.

Fogel stood up. A chest pain.

"Where are you going?"

"I'll be back in a minute."

"Are you all right?"

"I'll be back in a minute." The room was too big, high-ceilinged. A painted box with survivors scattered across the bottom. He almost ran out of it, dodging among the tables, bumping against a waiter carrying a loaded tray, roast Long Island duckling Montmorency. The waiter caught his balance, juggled the tray, steadied it; the dishes didn't spill on the carpeted floor; the ducklings were not wasted; they did not die in vain.

Outside the room: the lobby, made of marble. The chairs were tapestry, the ceiling, gilt plaster. Three rich women walked by—de la Renta, an Oscar de la Renta dress on one, Dior, Halston, one of those, an original. It made Fogel feel sick. Too much. There was too much here, layer upon layer upon layer. He was tired of New York, he wanted something simpler: green, light, old-fashioned, the wooden towns he had seen in his childhood, living ducks, air.

Fogel walked out of the front door of the Plaza past the uniformed guard. A prison, but this time with waiters. With smoked salmon, duckling. All the mattresses and pillows, room service, three meals a day, Plaza meals. For the survi-

9

vors, would it be enough? The park was what he needed. There was a duck pond down there, a little bridge, nature, simplicity, a garden, trees and water, air: Eden.

But now it was all black. Black trees arched over his head. A black path led down toward the water. It was so dark the path looked clean. But was it safe? He didn't dare walk on it. A man who had survived Bergen-Belsen, why should he be afraid? Why should it matter to him?

Fogel hurried away from the park entrance, back to the street, the public sidewalk, Central Park South, a fine place, airy also. He could lean on the stone wall and look down on the park. The cars driving behind him, the lights of the Plaza—these made him feel calm. But not his stomach, not the region near his heart. He was worried. Would he throw up his quenelles, his one bite, over the wall into the park?

Nothing was enough. It wasn't enough. All the avocados, all the silks, all the music, all the women, all the reds, the silvers, the $37.50 a couple, all the bombes glacées—it wasn't enough. It was too much. For anybody, for any person in history, it wasn't enough. He leaned over the stone wall, tears came out of his eyes, he began to gag. Then he sensed it, then he felt it, then he could see it: A black man was walking along the sidewalk toward him, black and shabby, a football player, a basketball player. An ominous sight. He was coming closer. Quick, Fogel, back to the Plaza! One mugging, and finished! Who would know, who would care? Who was listening, who was watching? Again the twentieth century rushes by while a man is getting killed.

Hurriedly Fogel pushed his hand into his pocket. Too much, more than enough, too much, his insides were disappearing. Once again he felt himself gagging. He caught his breath. Out of his pocket he pulled his handkerchief and spit into it, once to get the taste out of his mouth and then twice more—three times for good luck, a grandmother's superstition, foolish. Cautiously, he turned his head to look over his shoulder. The black man wasn't to be seen. No mugger, no nigger, no kapo, no Nazi, no killer, no Totenkopf.

But he felt dead. His mouth tasted of iron; there seemed to be a band of metal around the root of his tongue. With his hand pressed against his head, he leaned against the park wall, perhaps for five minutes, perhaps for two minutes. There was such a thing as a heart attack. Was there also such a thing as a head attack? Below him, in the duck pond, black waters flowed. Graveyard words flowed in his head. *Yisgadal. Yisgadash.*

Bracing himself against the wall, Fogel exhaled and then turned slowly to face the Plaza. With his handkerchief, he dabbed at his shirt and brushed his jacket lapels. In the glittering, bone-white men's room, he rinsed out his mouth. He washed his face. When he got back to his table, coffee had already been served. The lights had dimmed. The necrology was being read.

"*Where were you?*" A frantic whisper from his wife. "I sent Abe after you to the men's room, but you didn't answer."

"Sh!" Fogel said. "Sh!"

So many survivors had died this year. It was a bad year. The necrology rolled on, five minutes, ten minutes, the master of ceremonies, his voice swollen with portentousness, reading off the names. They traveled through the coils of the microphone, through the wires to the speaker system, and out, metallic, disintegrating into waves, into the air of the Plaza to mix with its food smells and perfumes.

June 23: Hannah Kalb, North Miami Beach, Florida, age seventy-two, originally Czernowitz. July 1: Herschel Zussman, Rego Park, age fifty-eight, originally Lodz.

11

"Are you all right? Where did you go?" Fogel's wife was staring at him.

"Sh. Sh."

"Are you all *right*?"

"I'm trying to listen."

Here, with this group, the necrology was unusual. It wasn't alphabetical; it was by date of death. Either they didn't know which alphabet to use or they despaired of finding the proper order for names like these—Polish, Romanian, Czech—beginning sometimes SZ, sometimes SH, sometimes TS, sometimes Z. So they did it by date. That also seemed appropriate. Days had retained their identities in the camp, people had not.

"September fourth." Very softly, behind the MC's rich voice, the band played Beethoven's "Funeral March." "Walter Frucht, Maplewood, New Jersey, age sixty-eight. September twenty-third, Yom Kippur, ladies and gentlemen: Eva Weintraub of Manhattan, age sixty. Originally Czernowitz also. A very pious woman."

He was getting up toward October 15, this day. Fogel put his hand on his neck, but his fingers had no feeling. The pain in his head had gone away. Its disappearance frightened him. Was he sitting down or standing up? He could be lying stretched out with candles at his head and at his feet.

"September twenty-fifth: Frieda Schoff.

"October eighth: Szymon Soless.

"October ninth: Pittel Gewirtz."

Or with a black prayer book placed in his hand.

"October eleventh: Herman Asch, Forest Hills."

Or a white flower.

"And just today. Just today, ladies and gentlemen. Just today. October fifteenth."

Wildly Fogel reached out to hold on to something, to the

12

side of the table, to the chair. He knocked a knife down. It went clattering to the floor.

Lillian whipped around, she put her hand on his face. "What's the matter with you?"

"Ladies and gentlemen, we have just received word of the sudden passing of another survivor." The MC made his voice especially somber: a death so fresh. "October fifteenth. Just today."

Fogel squeezed his wife's arm tight with all his strength.

"Theodore Mell of Kew Gardens, originally Warsaw."

Fogel's breath escaped out of him, a rattling gasp. Slowly, with effort, he unclamped his stiff fingers, he let go of his wife's arm.

So it was enough.

His name hadn't been called.

So it was enough. The others: They were enough.

He tumbled forward to lean against the table. His arm pushed against coffee cups, against a bonbon dish. He laid his head down on the table, he started to cry.

All the Jews, mourners, scattered across the room, stood up in the dim light to begin the recitation of the mourners' prayer, the master of ceremonies resonantly calling out the first words: Magnified and sanctified! Magnified and sanctified be the Great Name of the Lord! Only Fogel, crying, his fists against his eyes, he was the only one, only he didn't stand up.

That's the way it was every year. Always, there were one or two who couldn't bring themselves to stand up and praise God.

II

I am The Author. I am The Creator. I am The Omnipotent. I am The Omniscient. And, sometimes, I am The Merciful.

I determine who shall live and who shall die—who by starving and who by eating, who by Germans and who by headaches. I am the one who writes it in the book; and at the end I alone write the word "finished."

Fogel finished? A man who cries tears is not finished; nor a man who embraces his wife after he has cried tears; nor a man who eats both bran flakes and fried eggs for breakfast the morning after a banquet, having eaten little at the banquet itself; nor a man who puts aside the Sunday *Times* in order to revise his lecture on Frederick the Great. Finished? No, not finished. I am The Author.

I know who stands up to praise and who begins to stand and then suddenly sits down again. I am always watching, always listening. Fogel and Lillian, Steven and Marlene—I hear their voices. I see their deeds. As you read these pages, I read their hearts. I write the words they speak and the words hidden within their hearts, their secret, never-spoken words.

I form light. I create darkness. It is night. The telephone is ringing.

14

One ring. Now Fogel was more tranquil, now less fearful. Enough! Too much. Enough! Why anxiety? Why trauma feelings? Why fear? A second ring. No, a man should go about his work, ignoring emotional outbursts, his own as well as others', tending his own garden, devoting himself to the little plot life had allotted to him. A fourth ring. Lillian had not yet answered. Five rings. Slowly, Fogel put his copy of *Enlightenment Studies* facedown on the sofa and walked into the kitchen to answer the telephone.

His daughter Marlene nervously blurted out the good news.

"You can't do this to me," Fogel said. "This I don't need."

"I'm not doing it to you. I'm doing it to me."

Mrs. Revere Garrison Jessep. What a name! It sounded like Park Avenue. But upper Park Avenue, 125th Street, 130th Street. Every day on the train Fogel rode by those black tenements, and as he rode, he averted his eyes.

Lillian ran up the stairs to listen to her daughter on the bedroom telephone. After the telephone call was over, she walked down the stairs, very slowly. "No, no, no, no, no," she cried. Tears were running down her cheeks. Fogel went up to her. He put his arms around her. She pushed him away. "No!" she said again. "No! No! No! No, no, no, no, no!"

But the next morning at the breakfast table, Lillian sounded as if she were trying to adjust to this tragedy. "Maybe we should give her a nice wedding," she said. Her face was white from the strain of saying what she was saying.

"Are you crazy?" Could Fogel so easily adjust? Never! A daughter who would willingly go to bed with a Gentile, furthermore a black man. A daughter who already had, perhaps. A daughter who betrays millions of murdered Jews, many

15

her own relatives, by choosing such a marriage. "Believe me," Marlene had said, "very deep inside I know I'm doing the right thing." Fogel could hear his daughter's breath; on the extension he could hear Lillian's breath too. "Here." Marlene's voice was loud. "Here, I'll put Teddy on the phone." "No," Fogel whispered. "Not this time. Next time I'll talk." And Lillian could speak so, of a nice wedding, although the previous night after the phone call from Boston her crying had erupted so loud you'd think the neighbors would hear—crying, weeping, sobbing in bed in the middle of the night after Fogel was already asleep. She woke him up, crying from deep inside, wave after wave—no man could ever last that long at it. Again Fogel took her in his arms; again he tried to comfort her, stroking her back; clumsily he put his hands on her wet cheeks. She moved away angrily. She shook him off.

"No wedding," Fogel said. "No spending. Not a nickel, not a penny. Even if they paid me, no wedding, even for a million dollars, no." Here indeed: finished!

But now, the next morning after breakfast, Lillian was adjusting. She came into the bathroom while Fogel stood in front of the mirror shaving. "Maybe a nice wedding?" she said again.

Fogel pulled at his jawbone skin to facilitate under-chin shaving. In the mirror behind him, Lillian's face was misty. "Let me hear you answer," Lillian shouted, as if answering was easy over the Norelco-sound. As if hearing was easy. Fogel clicked off his razor switch. "A man and a woman!" Lillian was still shouting even though the razor had been turned off. "A man and a woman, no matter who they are, they deserve some respect. Don't you think I'm right? It's just the two of them. Marlene and Teddy. What does it have to do with anyone else?"

16

"Marlene and Teddy," Fogel repeated. In his mouth, each name tasted like sour fruit, even his daughter's name, even Marlene. For shame, thus to turn against his own child! Nevertheless, sour. The truth is the truth.

Lillian tried to smile. Then she repeated the name of the betrothed. In her mouth, the name seemed to pick up a little flavor, as if it weren't sour but maybe merely not-yet-ripe fruit. "Teddy," she said again. "Teddy." It was as if someday, almost, she would relish it.

Evidently he was called Teddy. He was named Revere, but called Teddy, why no one knew. Fogel didn't care why. He busied himself with his styptic pencil, whitening a bloody spot where he had cut himself on the throat. Yes, even with an electric razor, a man can draw blood.

Steven, the bride's brother, called from California, station to station, collect. His parents were already in bed for the night. "Mazel tov!" he said. "Wonderful, that's wonderful news." Until recently, Steven had been dangerously left. How long ago had it been that, in his father's presence, he had dared to refer to the Angela Davis trial as genocidal? But now he was turning away from politics; he was engaged in making a film on Zen meditation. "Where is the wedding going to be? What kind is it going to be? I could shoot it for course credit. What kind of film, indoor or outdoor?"

"What are you asking me for?" Trivial and insolent questions while Fogel's grandchildren were turning black. "How do I know? Inquire of the bride. What does it matter?"

"Indoor." Lillian had run downstairs to pick up the phone in the kitchen. "Indoor. A nice wedding. I'm going to make some phone calls tomorrow. I'll check prices."

Without saying good-bye, Fogel hung up the bedroom telephone.

"Come down to the kitchen now," Lillian shouted up the stairway. "I'm going to telephone Marlene."

"Late!" Fogel yelled back at her. "Late! Night-time! Late!"

"For us it's late. For them it isn't late."

Fogel put on his slippers and his blue winter bathrobe and walked downstairs to the kitchen. Lillian's hair was tangled. "Don't you think I hate it?" she said. Her cheeks were sagging. "Don't you think I'm not sick about it? My mother would die." Lillian's mother already had died: cancer. Her father had died too: emphysema. "But Marlene's our child. We have to accept it. We have to!" Lillian shut her eyes. "I'm going to call now. You hold my hand."

What good a telephone call? What good conversation, communication? What difference could they make? But these were considerations that did not restrain Mrs. Lillian Fogel. "Ted," Lillian cooed into the telephone. "Ted or Teddy, which is it?" Sitting next to her at the kitchen table, not holding her hand, his head aching from heart-strain, Fogel watched Lillian's mouth moving. Asking Marlene this question cost forty-five cents per minute. "Does Teddy have a car? Wouldn't he like to go for a little drive? Why don't you come home for the weekend? I'd love to meet him. I'd love to."

Maybe next time. Teddy wasn't ready. Still, Marlene could be convinced to come home—just to have a "nice little talk."

OUTSIDE THE Port Authority bus station, Marlene settled herself into the backseat while Fogel, shivering in the November wind, hoisted her suitcase into the car trunk. In the glare of the Eighth Avenue streetlights, Marlene's cheeks seemed as pale as Fogel's. But it was only because of the evil lighting.

18

"Such bright skin!" Fogel used to say when she was a little girl. "Such pretty color. A rose."

"Why not three in front? I'll move over." Lillian turned in her seat to face Marlene. "I'll sit in the middle. There's plenty of room." Marlene was on the small side like her Fogel relatives, now dead. But like them also, she was on the stubborn side. "No. Let's wait till we get home before we really have a talk."

Fogel also was on the stubborn side, insisting that his children remain Jews. Nix on intermarrying! Does not intermarrying destroy generations of Jews? Should the Jewish people die out? No, the Jewish people should survive! So, Hitler, see who triumphs in the end! Therefore, nix! Lillian had held on to Marlene before getting into the car, hugging her, kissing her, squeezing for seconds, for a minute, while taxi-horns assaulted Fogel's ears. To Lillian, what did that matter? Let time reel on! Emotions! Generations! Love! Hugging! Kissing! There were tears in Lillian's eyes. But there were none in Fogel's eyes. Nor did Fogel hug. Fogel merely kissed, if you call lips closed, chilly, brushing against a daughter's cheek, a kiss.

"Is Ted someone you'd consider a warm person?" Now Marlene was sitting in the dining room in White Plains leafing through a book, *The Letters of Eldridge Cleaver,* while her mother zealously tried to share the joy of the occasion. "Does he laugh a lot? Tell jokes?"

"His name is Teddy."

"Ted, Teddy, what difference does it make?" With a courtly bow to his daughter and another bow to his wife, with an equally courtly "Good night," with all deliberate speed, Fogel walked out of the room.

It is late, eleven o'clock. It is very quiet. Fogel's heavy

19

footsteps can be heard on the stairway and in the upstairs hall. Fogel's closing of doors can be heard, his running of water. A distant creaking noise can be heard: Fogel the father, Fogel the husband lying down on the marital bed.

Lillian stood next to the dining-room buffet, looking into her silver drawer: the pattern Rococo Dream. One day it might grace the Jessep dining table.

"Does Teddy show a lot of consideration for your feelings?" Lillian picked up a silver serving spoon to feel its weight. "Have you . . . ? I don't think I should ask this. It's none of my business. Have you gone all the way with him?"

"Of course we've gone all the way."

"Did you find it any different?" Tactfully Lillian looked down at the spoon in her hand. "Why should there be any difference? People are all the same, right?"

Marlene pushed her chair back abruptly and stood up. "I'm going to get a pen." As she left the room, her fist clenched and unclenched, then it clenched again.

"Of course it's different." Marlene walked back into the dining room. Her hips swayed subtly. "I never slept with anyone else I intended to marry." She sat down again and energetically began underlining a passage in the book.

How dark is Teddy? Answer: medium dark. How does he wear his hair? Answer: a moderate Afro. What does he look like? Answer: Thin-lipped, handsome. How tall is he? "No picture? You don't have a picture?" As if Lillian were astonished, as if she really wanted to look, to see him. As if she wouldn't want to take the picture and tear it to shreds. As if she wouldn't sit down on the floor and start mourning. Him too. Lillian and Fogel, both of them ignoring Marlene until night fell and she was swallowed up by darkness; she would disappear along with Teddy, exterminated.

20

Teddy, it turned out, was on the short side, like Fogel himself. This was the first good sign.

"Does he have a big family? What does his father do?"

"His father is employed by the Boston transportation system."

Jessep, the trolley motorman. Oh, the jokes the poor man had suffered! Teddy had reported some of them. Off the track, on the track. Ding, ding, there's a job with no future, lots of ahead, but no future. Couldn't he have worked his way up to the El? At least he wasn't demoted to the subway. "The Boston transportation system," Marlene said again sedately.

But Teddy himself was a graduate of the Boston Latin School and Tufts College. He had published three chapters of his dissertation. He already had his Ph.D. His grandfather had been the principal of a grammar school. His mother was a piano teacher. One of his cousins announced the weather on a Boston TV station. At Latin School, he had won the Approbation Prize. He had won the Fidelity Prize too. He knew Hebrew words: *kosher, shalom*; he had learned *tsuris, meshugge, mazel tov*. He was a man nobody had to apologize for. Nobody could third-degree him the way Marlene was being third-degreed. He'd know how to deflect it. It wasn't as if he had no background or achievements. If he were white there wouldn't be questions. If he were a Jew, there wouldn't be questions.

"Mommy!" Marlene suddenly cried out. She shut *The Letters of Eldridge Cleaver*. She stood up. She held her hand out as if she were trying to grasp on to Lillian. "Mommy! I can't stand this."

Lillian pushed the silver drawer closed. Tears blurred her eyes. "Do you think I enjoy it?" She moved away from Marlene toward the kitchen door. "I'm going to get a tis-

21

sue." She walked out of the room. In a minute she was back with a yellow box of tissues in her hand. Marlene was welcome to cry too.

Marlene sat down again. "Do you think I'm marrying Teddy because I want to rebel? I'm not a rebel. I'm a nice Jewish girl." She gave *The Letters of Eldridge Cleaver* a shove. The book went sliding away across the dining table, spinning precariously close to the table edge. "If I were marrying him just to rebel, he wouldn't even be interested in me."

Lillian didn't answer. She remained standing next to the table with the tissue box in her hand.

"Teddy's a professor," Marlene said. "He's had a middle-class upbringing."

Lillian's mouth stayed tight, but her eyes flickered. She pulled out one of the dining chairs—a chair with tweedy red-orange upholstery, blotched with pale spots where stains used to be—and sat down opposite Marlene.

"I was taking his course, 'Twentieth Century Urban Problems,' and one day—" Marlene blinked. "One day he came up to me after class and he wanted to talk to me about the Holocaust. Because of Daddy."

"How did he know?"

"It came up in a class discussion." With her ring finger, Marlene began rubbing the table. She wasn't wearing an engagement ring. "And everybody started looking at me like I was made out of glass. Like I could break." Marlene rubbed as if there were a dirty spot on the table. "They looked right through me."

Lillian reached across the table to pick up Marlene's hand. "Don't keep rubbing," she said. "You'll rub the polish off." She didn't let go of Marlene's hand.

"But Teddy never looked at me like that." With her other hand, Marlene started twisting a strand of hair around her finger, as tightly as if she were trying to kink it. "So we went to this coffee shop and we were eating Danishes and stuff like that and I was talking Holocaust; and Teddy just kept sitting there and listening, and then he said, 'I want to take you somewhere'; and he took me onto the subway and we got off at the Boston Common. And do you know where he took me to?" Marlene stopped short.

"You're the one who knows answers. Not me." Lillian let go of Marlene's hand. "I don't know answers."

"He took me into this little street, to in front of this old brick house where his great-great-something grandfather lived, and they had this pogrom there, this pogrom against blacks, and he was killed."

Lillian took a tissue out of the box and dabbed it against her eyes. "Whose pogroms do you want to cry for, theirs or ours?"

"A pogrom is a pogrom," Marlene said. After a moment, Marlene reached for a tissue too, but she used it for her fingers, not for her eyes: She began shredding it. "Then while we were just standing there looking at the house ..." Her voice began to waver. "He leans over and kisses me, and after he kisses me, he starts talking with this fake darky accent. 'I sho' be glad,' and 'You dig?' and all that stuff." Marlene plucked out another tissue. She began shredding that tissue too. "I told him to stop talking like that. Talk normally! He really talks with a Boston accent. Park your car. Harvard Yard." As she pronounced the words, Marlene scanted her Rs. "He shouldn't talk like some disk jockey in—in Alabama."

"What about him?" Lillian jerked her head upward, ges-

turing toward the place where Fogel was lying in bed un-
sleeping, breathing Fogel breaths. But for how much longer?
Thinking Fogel thoughts. But to what end?

Marlene jerked her head upward too. "He ought to understand," she said sharply. "He ought to sympathize. He's
not the only one who's been persecuted for no good reason."
With her hands she began sweeping tissue shreds together
into a little pile. Tears began weighing down Marlene's voice.
"Of course Teddy wasn't ever persecuted. He never had
such a hard time. You think black, so you think Harlem.
You think drugs, you think cleaning women. But Teddy
doesn't come out of Harlem. There's education in his family.
They're middle class. Boston blacks are middle class. All
these southern blacks are moving up to Boston now, and
he's trying to integrate them into the community. That's
what he wants to do and that's what I want to do too. That's
what Urban Studies is, for God's sakes!" Marlene took another tissue out of the box and wiped her eyes. Now she was
crying. "And I love him and I'm going to marry him and I
don't care what you think."

"Don't you care even about Daddy?"

Upstairs Daddy's bed creaks. Daddy tries to shut his eyes
even tighter. This time not a knife-headache. This time a
kick-headache. With such a headache, no man can sleep,
even a man who has managed to fall asleep beside corpses
in moving and then not-moving and then moving-again box-
cars. Not only is Daddy turned and tossed by headache; he
is turned and tossed by a suffering child, a child weeping
with her mother downstairs in the dining room. Should not
a father whose daughter-love encompasses also dead-sister
love, as well as dead-mother love—should not such a father
accept with gratitude whatever his daughter chooses to do?

Yes, he should accept.

24

No, he should not accept.

Finished, a daughter.

Finished also, a son! Steven also! Is it not true? Had not Steven once, when a senior at NYU, brought home a certain girl-visitor, a girl whose father had also come from Poland after the war, but a Gentile girl. The morning after that visit, had not Steven, sitting in the kitchen at breakfast time, blushed red, the color of shame? "I thought you'd be interested." Certainly, he himself had been interested, fondling the back of the girl's neck, touching her all the time. "If not interested"—with his spoon Steven had stirred his bowl of Wheatena, a bowl already well-stirred—"if not interested, at least polite."

Lillian, stern-faced, had unscrewed a syrup-jar cap so that her son could sweeten his cereal. "Your father was polite! Do you think he is like them?"

And had not Steven once, during a religion-discussion stroll with Fogel, answered only, "Beats me," after Fogel, a man who had read Spinoza and the *Dialogues* of Hume attentively, asked him, "How Jews without religion? How Jews without God?" *Beats me!* And when Fogel had further instructed him: "This is a paradox you must solve, little Jew. How? By having a Jewish wife and Jewish children. By following foolish customs, circumcision, snip, snip," easing the lesson by running his hand lightly across Steven's blue denim jacket. Had Steven, the son of a survivor, then answered: Of course! Yes! Certainly! Not to worry. Sh'ma Yisrael! Did Steven say these words? No, he did not.

Instead he said this: "What if I don't marry a Jew? What if I marry for love?" And then he said this: "More Jews, more victims."

"Quiet!" Fogel shouted at him. "Quiet, more victims!"

And then had not Fogel, quiet himself, walking ahead,

seen lying on the ground a fallen leaf, yellow as a star, and had he not picked it up and pressed it onto Steven's jacket, saying, "Only a Jew! Only a Jew!"

And had not the leaf, though damp, fallen off Steven's jacket?

And then, as if to apologize, had not Steven placed his hand on his father's arm and mumbled, "Only a Jew." So students mumble when they give incorrect answers! And then, as formerly when he was a little boy playing United States Army, summoning General Fogel to join him in his pretend-fort made from a big dishwasher box, had not Steven swiveled on his heels and saluted his father: "Yes, sir!" and then winked? A United States soldier, perhaps a British soldier like the one who had lightly touched Fogel's face with his fingertips on the day the British soldiers came to liberate Belsen.

On the street, Steven salutes and winks. In the dining room, Marlene rubs her fists against her eyes. "I love Teddy," she says. "You have to accept it." Upstairs Fogel can hear the sound of her voice. What matter if her words can't be heard? All are the same word: Finished.

Lillian heard the words. Her face seemed suddenly to slouch. "God keeps himself busy arranging marriages." This was what Lillian's own mother, now resting in peace, had said when Lillian had come home to Walton Avenue with the news: Fogel had proposed and she had accepted. On that day, her mother and her father, a presser with cigarette-yellowed fingers, had sat on either side of her on the living-room studio couch under the tulip wallpaper and had hugged and kissed her. They hadn't objected to Fogel. On the contrary, they had been pleased: a professional man.

Lillian picked up another tissue and held it ready in her hand. "Just make sure you raise your children as Jews," she said. "Just Jews. For your father. Replacements. That's all I ask. Jews." Then she brushed the tissue against her eyes.

Marlene crumpled the tissue in her own hand and then put it onto the pile of shredded tissues. "I've already broached the subject to Teddy."

"What did he say?"

"He didn't say no."

"Were you thinking in terms of"—Lillian almost began to smile—"a big wedding or a small one?"

"Teddy's parents want us to get married quietly," Marlene said nervously. "They're embarrassed."

"That's terrible! If that's what they think, how do they expect us to think any differently?" Lillian's eyes narrowed. "I'd be willing to have a big wedding, invite everyone, the St. Moritz maybe. But your father, no. He's embarrassed. That's where your problem is."

"Ain't my problem, baby." All of a sudden, Marlene's voice was transformed, husky, richly patterned. "That his problem." She had an impeccable Negro accent.

"Don't worry." Lillian was whispering. "I'll fix it. He's nervous, listen, you can't blame him, it hasn't been easy for him, you could have considered it." She leaned forward. The edge of the dining table pressed into her flesh painfully. "Just imagine what you'd like most. Tell me exactly what you want. Describe your ideal wedding."

III

A spring wedding, that was it.

A bridal gown from Priscilla of Boston.

For the big things, the important things, it's best to be traditional. "If I weren't going to be traditional," Marlene said, "we'd just live together. Why get married?"

Sunday, April the Seventeenth, Nineteen Hundred and Seventy-three at Two in the Afternoon.

The roof of the St. Moritz.

The first truly integrated wedding in the history of Central Park South.

A white came in to make the reservation and pay the deposit. But half the guests were black.

The only inconvenience: too many klieg lights.

Sanford S. Kashroff, Hillel rabbi at the Free University of Boston, performed the ceremony through the authority vested in him by the State of New York. When the groom stepped on the wineglass and shattered it, Solomon and Sheba embraced again in heaven. I am black but comely, the groom told himself. Black is comely.

The Jesseps had once attended an Africa-style ceremony, non-Christian, with juju idols in the corner, candles burning, little baby dolls from the five-and-ten scattered in front of

28

the bride and groom, rice poured through fingers. But this was a first.

And for Teddy, an eye-opener. So what! Every groom is a stranger at his own wedding.

There was a Jewish band, there was dancing. When the bride and groom did the Ape, to the tune of "Havah Nagilah," Jews and blacks together, clapping hands in a circle around them, no question about it: They both had rhythm. All the landlords in Harlem should have seen it, all the tenants, the ADL, the JDL, the Panthers, the PLO: It was beautiful. Clapping, left and right, sway; little girls went twirling into horas inside the circle. How the blacks whooped and cheered when one cousin from Hewlett, Long Island, crouched down and did a kazatsky for three, four minutes. That's what wins wars, that's what beats Arabs; that's what knocks out their tanks and bombers before they're close enough to Jerusalem to smell the chicken soup cooking. A beautiful time was had by all.

The movie—Steven's final version—begins like this:

Teddy's finger, held out rigid, with a gold wedding band being slipped onto it by Marlene. You see her little white fingers gingerly holding the ring, slipping sweetly up his finger. In on the ring, in on the ring. There's nothing to see but light reflecting on gold (fortunately, a broad band) and then out to the two of them dancing cheek to cheek; not them exactly, but their cheeks only, one black, one white.

Out then to include all of them. A play with the wedding finery. How white the bridal gown is, how soft; how black the groom's tuxedo, unrelieved black, total, a statement.

Guests. First the black guests, eight or ten of them, very still-like objects. Then the white guests.

Lillian, mother of the bride, you will live again on film.

Fogel, father, I have saved you out of the fire for this.

29

Now your bones can fall away. For this, the God of Abraham, the God of Isaac, the God of Jacob carried you out of Europe. For this, your grandfather and his grandfather marched in procession around My ark, bearing myrtle, palm and willow in their hands, and unblemished citrons. For this they chanted, "Save us! Save us!"

Papa Jessep, Mama Jessep! Out of the chains, the coffles, out of the prisons, out of Shango and Shigidi, you have been brought to this.

Lillian: For four years she had eaten nothing but apples and cottage cheese for lunch; still she wasn't happy with her body. At the ceremony, she looked sagging, past menopause. Her daughter with the black man—that was where the juice was; and with the black mama, her dress red, her heart black.

A shot of the two mothers: the handshake, the embrace, one with arms around the other. Mrs. Jessep: a swinger. Elora, it didn't take her long to learn the hora. A heavy woman, but light on her feet. Admit it, Lillian: It would take you a month to learn Motown rock and even then you wouldn't be good at it.

A long camera exploration of the Afros, up and down little valleys, around whorls, over ridges, through the jungle tangle into the depths; and then in counterpoint, the straight, gleaming, sheeny black of the Jews' hair. The bride's hair, camera sliding up and down. Sequins on the gowns glittering, silver and black. The texture of liquor in the glasses. The glasses themselves.

Preoccupation with objects. One of Steven's professors had given warning: It was bad cinematically, counterproductive in terms of content, counterrevolutionary actually. More than one Ph.D. in Cool Media had been known to end up filming TV commercials. A dire prediction, but here it didn't matter; here social content was intrinsic in filmic content. This was

30

a commercial for the brotherhood of man, a montage of black on white on black on white on black on white.

The camera took a little tour around heads of hair again. A quick jump over Fogel's balding, graying head. *Afrodisia,* the title. It could have commercial possibilities. Cannes! Cannes! The Gold Laurel. *Ghetto Wedding.* Another title. Black face against white face; black hand shaking white hand; lips, thick and thin, kissing. Bone structure: chinbones, jawbones, cheekbones. An inspiration: large breasts where the bride and groom had suckled. First to the mother-in-law and then quickly, almost embarrassedly, to ample Lillian. (Steven himself had been bottle-fed, and not on demand either.) A fortunate visual accident on one side of the room: six, eight breasts lined up. A shy look at the bride, zoom. Teddy's eyes, in close. Teddy's hands, brown and veiny; Teddy's mouth, open up, Teddy, let's get a little nip of the teeth. The folds made by thighs in the bridal gown as the bride dipped and danced, white satin rippling this way and that over the place where the future of the world would come forth: numerous children, middle-colored, future-colored.

"In film, as in all art," Steven's professor had said, "there is no past, only present." Nevertheless it was wrong to edit the Jesseps and Lillian out of the film, to cut every shot of Fogel, casting his picture onto the floor: Fogel sternly kissing his daughter, Fogel awkwardly dancing with Teddy's mother, Fogel pinching his lower lip while the rabbi joins Revere and Marlene in marriage. Only shots of the bride and groom? That was too chaste, artistically.

This was not in any way a chauv ceremony. Marlene insisted that all the singles, including males, stand around to catch the bridal bouquet. A beautiful scene: blacks, whites, youths, maidens; even the homely ones were beautiful; Teddy's cousin, the one who needed orthodontia; Cousin Melvin, the Macy's salesman—even these. The camera paired them off—this one with that—and then it played switches, more careful to end up white-black than boy-girl. An orgy. "Wait, wait," Steven called out. Marlene was about to throw the bouquet. "You." He pointed to a white girl he didn't know. "Go up and kiss Teddy." She did it. "You now." He pointed at his cousin Melvin. "You too." The cousin looked at Steven as though he were crazy. Teddy laughed, Marlene laughed, the youths and maidens, most of them, laughed too. In this crowd Melvin was more afraid of being considered a racist than a queer; he went up and put his arm awkwardly around Teddy. Teddy recoiled. A loud, fake smack of the lips: Melvin pretended to kiss. It can be seen on film.

Ruthie Faber, white, red hair, kissed Salton Wind, black, both Ph.D.'s. Joshua Schwartz put his arm around the bare brown shoulder of Grace Trowel; she leaned up and kissed him passionately, murmuring blackly, "Honey." Bonny Rosenfeld edged her way over to Diggy Ernest, away from Paul Lapidus. Later, Diggy took her home and really gave it to her. But that's another story, outside this frame. By the time Linda Savitz and Jojo Neat got ready, there were no youths left. The maidens shyly held each other's hands. Steven— his cup runneth over—zoomed in on them. What about you, Steve? What about you? And what about you, Fogel, father, standing angry outside the circle? You already have been indissolubly wed.

Marlene threw her bouquet straight at her brother.

He bobbled the camera, almost dropped it; with the camera in one hand, he caught the bouquet, which had landed on his chest.

He held it, frozen, one frame: a tintype.

Then who would it be? Grace Trowel? Jojo Neat? Dorothy Dandridge? Maybe even Linda Savitz?

Revere and Marlene Jessep ran out of the room. To go out as inconspicuously as possible, they took the service elevator down. Teddy was still wearing the gold-embroidered yarmulke which Rabbi Kashroff had ceremoniously placed on his head before the bride walked down the aisle. Lillian's Aunt Sarah-Who-Never-Shuts-Up had straightened out the yarmulke when she cornered Teddy, before Lillian came to his rescue with a smile and a wink and an excuse: "Teddy! Come, I have to introduce you to Irving." Irving had patted the yarmulke while he was handing Teddy a wedding gift—another envelope. Salton Wind, Teddy's best man, had removed the yarmulke and tried it on himself and then replaced it, while Teddy was discreetly pretending to sip his third drink. "Dis be it," Teddy said to Marlene while they were walking through the service corridor. He took the yarmulke off and put it in his pocket. "Dis be it. Get used to it. It de back elebator from now on."

Marlene pulled Teddy's head close to her own so she could whisper into his ear. Too serious for a bride beginning her honeymoon, too intense. "Listen, Teddy," she said, "listen to me. Don't ever play nigger at me again. I've already had enough of Oh-how-persecuted-we-have-been from my father."

"Headache!" At the head table, Fogel pressed his hand against his forehead. "Let's us go away also." He put his hand over his eyes, he rubbed the side of his head above the left ear.

"It's wrong." Lillian was shaking her head. "It's inappropriate."

"Headache. Too much. Also this wedding! It too is not inappropriate?"

"Don't you think I know that?" Again Lillian was shaking her head. "Don't you think I don't know. But you have to stay until the last guest leaves. You're the host."

"Maybe I could go lie down." With stiff fingers, Fogel tapped his forehead. "Then when the last guest is leaving, out the door, then I could come back."

"I'll ask a waiter for some aspirin." Throughout the room, waiters were clearing dishes from the tables, leaving only the centerpieces, little white vases filled with roses.

"A black headache. Iron."

Mrs. Jessep was walking around the room, pulling flowers out of vases, at one table after another. Fogel pointed at her. "You can forget aspirin. For this headache, aspirin won't work." Inside his head letters were twisting, forming large indecipherable black words. Mrs. Jessep arrived at a table nearby. "Little souvenirs," she called out, waving girlishly at her new relatives. "It's OK if I take them, right?" Lillian, the hostess, smiled at her. Fogel, the host, moaned. "Headache."

"Shhh!" Lillian hissed. "Shhh!"

"Don't tell me shhh, Lillian. Don't tell me thankful." Fogel was sitting at a table still decorated with flowers. "Don't tell me think: the no-weddings, the little girls, the without-weddings. Don't tell me my sister dead." Fogel pressed the palm of his hand against his forehead. "You shhh! Headache. This is what I tell you. Headache. What good aspirins? Let me tell you. Headache!"

34

IV

A student wrote a letter. "Dear Professor Fogel, If Voltaire was alive now, he would be assassinated. He would be a member of the pig establishment. Rousseau represents the wave of the future. Rousseau would be a Maoist today." It was unsigned. But Fogel could tell: The author was black. The world was being taken over by the colored races. Africans, Arabs, pagans—races untouched by modern scientific enlightenment. Voltaire's civilization was dying, Lessing's civilization—the antidote to Auschwitz—the civilization to which Fogel had devoted his life. Inferior ideals were taking its place. Had the Africans ever even invented the wheel?

Such thoughts! They made Fogel ashamed. He himself had once been an inferior. Sitting at his desk in the downstairs playroom, he unbuttoned his shirt cuff to see the numbers on his arm. A reminder: Mankind should be enlightened. Look at what ideas of racial and national superiority had led to! *Alle Menschen werden Brüder.* It was only hatred, race hatred—white against black, German against Jew—that brought evil. Arab against Jew; Christian against Jew; Ukrainian, Pole against Jew. Inferiors against superiors. Vice versa also. *Shvartzer.* Nigger. The words drummed at his mind. Why shouldn't he be a Nazi too?

For dinner Lillian served African peanut soup. "Deli-

35

cious," Fogel said, "very original." And politely he asked for a second helping.

"I started with whole peanuts, not peanut butter," Lillian explained happily. "It's made with the blender. When we go to the new club, I'll serve it."

"What new club?"

"The White Plains International Culinary Club. I joined us. An integrated group, six couples. Everybody makes one course. You'll love it."

"I have no desire to go." But Fogel licked his spoon. "International. Stupid!"

Why not keep eating? Has God accomplished it all yet? Fogel slid the spoon along the rim of the bowl to reach every drop. More babies have to be born; more wars have to be fought, international. More gassings, more starvings, more killings. More history majors, though there are fewer of those now; the jobs just aren't there, and what jobs exist are only for Americanists, maybe a medievalist or two. There are no new Enlightenment men; look at *Enlightenment Studies,* the same names over and over again: Scully at Northwestern, Kolb at Louisiana State, once a year in the journals. New names don't show up: no CCNY, no Hunter, no NYU even. They have an anti–New York bias, the board of editors. What sense to write a new paper? Maybe on Lessing's conception of death. Maybe on Lessing and Lavoisier, though this is more an episode in the history of science. A topic with a scientific turn might entice them. "Never mind." Fogel pushed his soup bowl away. "Already we know enough eaters." For Lessing: salons, philosophers, theatrical companies. For Fogel: eaters. With his fingernail, Fogel picked a peanut crumb out of his teeth. The soup hadn't been completely blended.

"I promised. One meeting. Maybe you'll like it. What's there to lose?"

36

"Not weight. Dollars, perhaps, but not pounds." A joke. Fogel grinned at Lillian, showing his teeth. They had out-lived Hitler. They would outlive even Fogel.

"African Culinary Club of White Plains, I won't go." Fogel repeated it in bed, this time in a whisper. America was blending and his own wife was pushing the buttons: Whip, chop, mix, mash, blend. "You go. You enjoy it. Your friends."

"Always the same thing." Lillian punched her pillow up against the headboard. "You don't want to go anywhere." She sat up and leaned back against the pillow. "Even before Marlene. Señor Complaint! This is no good, that is no good. Señor I-Don't-Want! Monsieur Headaches! What's the matter with you anyway, Chaim? What is it, male menopause?"

"I am dying."

"What do you mean? What are you talking about?" Lillian grabbed his shoulder. "What do you mean you're dying?"

"I am dying. I am going to die." Hitler exterminated only Jews. God exterminates everybody, animals, continents, even Hitler. For everybody, a final solution. Already Fogel was older than his father had ever been, his mother. You got more than me, pig. It was the voice of his sister, as if years were candy. What was Hitler compared to God? Fogel shut his eyes. The lamplight was too bright.

"What is it? You saw a doctor? He said something?" Lillian's nails dug into Fogel's skin. "Did a doctor say something? Don't they tell the wife?"

"I have no need to see a doctor. What could a doctor tell me?"

"What's the matter with you? Where do you hurt?"

"Everywhere."

"Show me." Click! Lillian switched the light higher. Click again!

"Here." Fogel pointed to his forehead. "Six months. Nine months. Here. Here. I have a headache."

37

"God!" Lillian raised her hands to her face. "We'll go right away, a specialist. The emergency room. Now. They'll give you tests. You'll go in."

"I am not going in." Fogel's eyes opened to the glare. "I am not going in."

"That's crazy. Tests, you need tests. Chaim!" She leaned over him. His eyes stared straight up, no longer looking at her, Widow Fogel. A corpse. This was farewell. "Chaim, listen to me. Chaim, don't be stubborn. Oh, Chaim." She leaned over him, she fell on him crying.

Is this a time for her to cry? It's Fogel who has the headaches. It's Fogel who'll be lying underground, Star of David Cemetery, Farmingdale, Long Island, while she's eating peanut soup, while she's dancing. "Older Singles, Over 35," it says in the newspaper ads. This could also mean over forty-nine. Fogel had seen her reading such newspaper ads. He had observed excitement-flush rising on her cheeks as she read. He had seen her smile at handsomes on the TV screen. And at handsomes in the shopping mall.

And now she was weeping. Absently he stroked her shoulder. What else could a man do?

Suddenly Lillian sat up. "Too hysterical!" She patted his hand and smiled. "Maybe it's psychosomatic. Did you take aspirin?"

Fogel nodded. Why answer with words? Talking also could make his head hurt.

"I don't believe it, Chaim. You're not dying."

"At the funeral you'll believe it. Already I'm a dead man."

The corpse rose, it sat on the side of the bed for a moment, it reached for its slippers, it padded off to the bathroom. When ghosts move, it's not into the bathroom. Ghosts don't flush. You don't hear the plumbing rattle through the house.

When Fogel crawled back into bed, Lillian leaned over

mournfully to kiss him on the forehead. "Do you think I'll sleep tonight?" She said it again the next night. "Do you think I'll sleep tonight either? If I didn't nap this afternoon, I'd be walking around dead myself."

BUT FOGEL SLEPT, except for one night, the night he dialed Boston to tell his daughter that she was giving him excruciating headaches. "Why worry her?" Lillian cried out. "Why? Especially now. Steven too. Why should they be worried?" Marlene's telephone rang, unanswered, at two A.M., and again at three A.M.; Steven's similarly at four A.M. But, except for that night, Fogel slept.

And in the daytime Fogel worked, sitting inside his carrel at the library, writing vicious notes on Fittbogen's *Die Religion Lessings,* a book he held in the utmost contempt. He lectured on the Enlightenment, congratulating his students on their good fortune: They were its heirs. He lectured on Voltaire, spicing the hour with suggestive references to Catherine the Great's admiration for eminent literary men. "This was not the same, I must remind you, as Catherine's admiration for other men." Lewd chuckles escaped him.

He rode through the Bronx on train tracks, past houses where Jews had once lived, where once, as they were commanded, they had hammered onto their doorposts the proclamation: God. The proclamations were still there, almost invisible under coats of paint, but the Jews had vanished as if the Angel of Death had flown over them. Blacks lived in their places.

Fogel is dying. The Jews are dying. The evil will has been accomplished. Steven Richard Fogel. Marlene Fogel Jessep. Fogel's grandchildren, the mixlings, never will they grasp the rooster around the neck, or the hen, and whirl it, calling out: This is my change, this is my compensation. This animal will die and I will live. Never, calling out to God for deliverance,

39

will they cast bread crumbs into the sea or the river, polluting them with the sins of redeemed Jews.

"Why don't you film these things, these ancient customs, before it is too late?" Fogel wrote to his son, his agonized cramped little letters dying on the page as the ink ran out of his ball-point pen. "Why are you filming Hare Krishnas? Why interracial, St. Moritz weddings? Why not film Jews? Remember the Jews before it is too late, capture these quaint customs on film, they are all disappearing. Why do you go to these rallies, these marches, these student demonstrations, and waste film on them? Are you CBS? Let NBC do that. You are something else: JEW. Film Jewish customs quickly before they wither away. If not, then give me your camera. I will make films. I also possess a visual imagination. You are a chip off my block. From me you inherited your eyes. Remember, I have lived this long only because I was a painter."

Not exactly an artist—this Steven knew—but a painter nevertheless; for twenty months in the work camp at Drohobych stenciling FORBIDDEN! onto signs, DO NOT ENTER! BEWARE, FIRE! in German, Polish, Ukrainian. "I have no craft," Fogel had confessed to his mother's cousin, after slipping away from Lvov (dangerous) to sneak in among the laborers at Drohobych (maybe not so dangerous).

The oil-refinery firelight flickering over the camp reddened the man's neck. "So, good-bye." He ran a finger across his throat.

"Then I will fabricate a craft." And he had invented a new person, Chaim Fogel, the sign-painter, a man who saw colors everywhere, not just the dark, ominous Nazi green of the signs he painted, not just the petroleum-flame color coming out of the refinery chimney, but also colors which lived in his brain; and afterward, first for the weeks his transport-

40

group waited at Auschwitz, and then for the months at Bergen-Belsen, where everything was monochromatic—uniforms, buildings, sky, earth, chimneys, faces, all things gray and lifeless as if they had already gone up in smoke: a rainbow. He envisioned his own eyes, green, suffused with light, shining like Jerusalem in heaven, like emeralds on the fingers of God; he saw his blood drops, his spit, his urine drops, his tears: pure color. Scum covered his teeth but inside was whiteness, a king's ivory palace. Sometimes, lying in the dark, he touched one of his fingernails with his tongue; this luxurious smoothness: pink. He made the camp-chill part of himself, as if his bones were—so beautiful!—ice-white; as if his heart and the cave of his belly were ice.

And now color was entering into his own family. So the God of the Jews had recompensed Fogel's color-thinking.

Once Fogel had ventured to go to a movie about a concentration camp. He had paid money to see—what? a travelogue!—dead space, mist. He himself could make such a movie, but it would not show the camp—only one picture: a square of matzoh, its ridges browned by fire, its dead-white places where the fire had passed over, its barbed-wire rows, endless, each dot in it a life. THIS IS THE BREAD OF AFFLICTION, a voice would call out, THE BREAD OF AFFLICTION OUR FATHERS ATE IN THE LAND OF EGYPT! And as the voice called out, cracks would appear in the bread of affliction, the bread of affliction would break into pieces, it would crumble, it would disintegrate into ashes, grains as numberless as the sands of the sea, each one an affliction. And the afflictions would disappear. They would go up in smoke, into heaven like the smoke of the burnt offerings. It is accomplished. Amen. Selah. The end. What is a few thousand years in time, what is a person in history, one life in a span of a few thousand years? A short subject.

41

The movie would be black and white, not color. Fogel's brain scanned by a machine and then displayed on a light box, was black and white too—actually black and gray, gray as Auschwitz or Bergen-Belsen. Unphotographed by the brain scan: any sign of headache-tumor, any indication of headache-growth. Fogel's EEG, black on white, showed only a jagged lifeline, wavering and uneven, but nothing unusual.

At Mount Sinai the doctor, a tall, bald man, looked happy. With his fingernails, he tapped the top of his desk. Fogel and Lillian leaned forward on orange plastic chairs. The room smelled of air-conditioning. Behind the doctor's head, diplomas covered the walls. "I don't find anything. It's not a tumor. Don't worry. Calm your mind."

From Lillian came a choking sound. "I'm so relieved. Oh, thank God! Thank God!"

"A brain tumor is a lump. This shows no lump. We can be thankful, the tests don't show anything. The brain scan would almost certainly show it. Nothing. There aren't any other indications. There's no erratic behavior, right?"

Fogel shook his head.

"God, no!" Lillian said.

"Then it's only headaches, right." The doctor switched off the light on the screen. Fogel's brain disappeared.

The doctor leaned forward, resting his elbows on the desk. "Has there been anything on your mind lately, anything upsetting you? That might explain your headaches?"

Fogel's head moved. Now instead of facing the doctor, he was facing the door, a door of opaque glass. Through it he had entered the office and through it he would depart. Into the brain they can look. Into the mind, no.

"Oh, yes! Our daughter." Lillian was watching the doctor as intently as Fogel was watching the door. "Very upsetting. An interracial marriage."

"Ah," the doctor said sorrowfully. "Ah."

In the car on the way home—this time Lillian drove—Fogel wriggled angrily in his seat. He unlatched his safety belt, the warning buzzed. *"Gowno!"* A Polish obscenity. He had never uttered it in front of Lillian. *"Gowno!"* Wisely, she didn't ask what he was saying.

Fogel's diagnosis: God is laughing. Recommendation: See a psychiatrist. Take aspirin.

"Psychosomatic, they make up the word, you make up the disease. At my age hypochondria isn't nothing." Rage made Fogel forget grammar. "A Nazi diagnosis!" The automobile was filled with the sound of buzzing. It made his head stop hurting, but only for a moment. What is one moment compared with all the others? A temporary illusion, a nothing. Fogel hit both fists against the dashboard. He lowered his head to rest upon his fists. The car jounced over a pothole. Fogel's head jounced against his fists. "Crash me," he said to Lillian. "Crash me." Such driving was hazardous. Fogel rebuckled his safety belt. "What does it matter, a crash?" He shut his eyes. "First the camps, now the headaches. God is making jokes at me. Maybe crashing is yet another joke."

Foolish man! I do not joke. I do not laugh. What I have promised I deliver, and what I deliver I have promised. Cf. Ezekiel, chapter V, verses 14–15.

Foolish man! As it is said, "Know what is above you—a seeing eye and a hearing ear, and all your deeds written in a book." Cf. *Ethics of the Fathers*, chapter II.

Foolish man! Not only all your deeds, but all your thoughts too, as it is written, "He knows the secrets of the heart." Not only all your thoughts, everything. Everything.

V

Headache in the morning. Headache at night. Headache lying down. Headache rising up. Headache sitting at home within the doorposts. Headache going about in the street. Headache like a seal between the eyes. In the psychiatrist's dark office on East Seventy-ninth Street, behind closed neuter-colored curtains which blocked out street noise, Fogel sat stiff-backed in a luxuriously soft chair, a big chair in which a man could easily relax if he weren't paying by the minute for the pleasure of sitting in it. At least NYU paid for half. The money went to Dr. Wax, a broad man, bushy-bearded, a man younger than Fogel, also taller, and wearing a tweed jacket as if he were the academic, not Fogel.

"Go," Lillian had said. "What harm can it do? Maybe it will help."

Should not Fogel, as Lillian had urged, be more open-minded? Might it not, as Lillian had suggested, prove to be an interesting experience? A fascinating experience? Perhaps even a helpful experience? Should not a historian guiding the next generation be familiar with the intellectual currents of his own time, e.g., Freudianism, as well as with the ideas of the past? Would not Voltaire so familiarize himself?

Would not Lessing? Would not Rousseau jump at the opportunity? Should not Fogel also jump?

When did the headaches start? How long did they last? Was there anything that set them off? Fogel was an intelligent man, a professor, able to analyze.

"Mr. Fogel."

"Dr. Fogel," Fogel said. "A Ph.D."

"Dr. Fogel, you're an enlightened man. I have a great deal of confidence in you." Dr. Wax's mouth smiled to indicate friendliness. Also at this time, his beard moved. "There's a lot we can do to get rid of your headaches. But I think it's unwise to put a man like you into deep analysis, to start looking at your childhood, that sort of thing. We have to deal with the here and now."

That was how Fogel became a member of a psychotherapeutic group—to cure headaches. A group even less appetizing than the White Plains International Culinary Club.

One more selection, but this one a small selection, six people, all of them sufferers already, sitting on a couch or on folding chairs in a carpeted office, talking to each other. Talking was supposed to end their suffering.

And who was among them? To Fogel's embarrassment, one of his students, not exactly a student, but maybe. A senior, Terry, a child Marlene's age, an almost plump girl, sturdy-looking with blonded, frizzy hair, a girl with a space between her two upper front teeth, therefore an oversexed girl.

"I know you!" Terry bounced in her chair. "I went to your lectures for almost a month. With a friend. He was in your course, and I was spending all my time with him."

"Which lectures did you attend?"

Terry bit her lip as if it were an examination and she was trying to concentrate. Then she shrugged.

45

Numerous lectures, but none of them she could remember.

"Weren't you going to your own classes? You should go instead to your own classes."

Terry responded to this with a wink.

Cancer was what had brought Terry to Dr. Wax's psychotherapeutic group.

"All my tests prove out negative. It's psychosomatic, in my mind." Terry tapped her head. The cancer was growing. It was reaching her arms. Every ache proved it: the toes, the breasts. Certainly it was cancer. Dr. Wax was working on a remission.

"In case his remission doesn't work, I'm having my aura fixed." Terry put her hands on her lap and closed her eyes. "I also do deep breathing." There was blue makeup on her eyelids. She took a deep breath and then let it out loudly. "Not real oxygen therapy, just breathing. You should try it."

"This you believe in? Breathing? Auras?" A typical student: a dreamer of dreams.

"You believe in Dr. Wax?" Again Terry tapped her head. Dr. Wax's reaction was to smile tolerantly.

Group member number one: Terry, imaginary cancer.

Group member number two: Schwartz, a freckled, red-haired man with a sexual-identity problem. This didn't mean that Schwartz disliked women. Schwartz liked women. However, also he liked women's clothing. He enjoyed dressing in skirts, in blouses. Once his wife had caught him putting on one of her brassieres. This was how he came to be in treatment with Dr. Wax. In treatment, that's what Dr. Wax's clientele called it. Fogel was in treatment.

"You think transvestites are funny." Schwartz was a big man talking angrily. Therefore, he could be dangerous. This

46

Fogel knew from his past life. "Most people think so. But for me it's not funny."

"I don't think it's funny." Fogel sat tightly in his chair. "Why should I think it's funny? I am a European. Therefore, I have seen worse." These words seemed to calm Schwartz.

Number three: Charlotte, also attractive, but older than Terry, a woman who suffered from panics in the subway. Taxis she couldn't afford; psychoanalysis she could pay for.

Number four: a jealous wife.

Number five: Macy, a thin young man with yellowed teeth, a boy actually, who made his living by working with computers. It was said that he had a brilliant future.

All of them Jews. Jews, Jews, Jews, Jews, Jews, Jews.

All of them also sickies! The number of divorces! The mothers they hated! The wicked fathers! How they chattered on and on only about their thoughts! Like birds. Not their ideas, their thoughts. "Be open-minded," Lillian had said on the first day Fogel visited Dr. Wax. "Be open-minded and learn." But none of them had ever even heard of Lessing.

Except maybe Terry. She wasn't sure. "I think you talked about him in a lecture. A French writer?"

But about Dr. Wax she was sure. "This is all crap," she said while she and Fogel were sitting in the waiting room the following week. Fogel nodded; he would be agreeable. "You're the only person in the group who sees eye to eye with me on that." Fogel smiled. His head stopped hurting. "I don't believe in any of it. Dr. Wax thinks he's God. That's why he grew his beard. The thing is . . ." Terry's dark eyes scuttered from side to side like mice, first one way, then back again. "My father pays for it. He

47

wouldn't pay to have my aura fixed. Or for reflexology. I'll try new things. He won't." She tugged at her hair and growled.

"Now YOU TALK," Dr. Wax commanded on the fourth Tuesday evening at 5:15 as all of them sat in a circle under the diplomas on the wall. "The group is like a new family, a helpful family. They'll listen and give you guidance. Some of their ideas may surprise you." Dr. Wax was not wearing his tweed jacket today; instead, he wore a blue blazer. "Or annoy you. But the more attention you pay to what the group says, the better off you'll be."

A new family! Inside his head, beneath the place where the ache was, Fogel began to laugh. But this was something they didn't know, they couldn't see, no matter how open-minded he was. All they could know was what he would tell them. Oh, what he could tell! What he could say! Why shouldn't he say? He said, "My daughter married black. Six months now, married, and my wife, to her it doesn't matter. Never mind my wife. Like you." Terry was looking at him intently, maybe not so bad, maybe a sweet girl, also suffering. "I have a terrible sickness, headaches, every day a headache. Bufferin, Excedrin, Darvon, Extra-Strength Anacin, you name it, it's all the same. Aspirin is like swallowing money."

"It's not physical," Dr. Wax said quickly. "There is no tumor."

"Worse than a tumor." Fogel rubbed his forehead. He was the only one there who didn't hate his mother. "My son is in California. I was in Bergen-Belsen." He stopped; he picked at the cane seat of his folding chair. The cane was coming loose. It was breaking. The chair would last maybe another six months, maybe a year.

"What's Bergman-Belsen?" Terry addressed the question

48

to Dr. Wax. Not to Fogel. Was Dr. Wax there? No, Fogel was there. Terry, an ignorant.

"Tell them."

"They don't know?"

Dr. Wax refrained from answering.

"Belsen, who doesn't know? Lessing, I can understand, nobody knows Lessing. Dr. Wax, you don't even know Lessing, I wouldn't be surprised. But Bergen-Belsen they should know. Jews. I won't tell them."

"You can't say it?"

"I can say it. Of course."

"Then say it." Dr. Wax smiled yet again. This smile was meant to be encouraging.

As Fogel had dragged bodies to the burial pits at Belsen to earn food, so Dr. Wax, also to earn food, was attempting to drag Fogel to talking. Did talking stop headaches? Not yet. Fogel sat squarely on his chair, his legs inflexible. Now let the chair break. Maybe its years were over. "They should already know. Let them read history books." History was carrying them, fast as a subway train. Last stop. All out. For this, should Fogel's eyes show tears? Certainly not! "I won't tell them."

Terry was blushing.

"My own father came from Vienna in 1938," Dr. Wax said modestly.

"Also Freud. Then you tell them."

"What's the mystery?" Charlotte, subway panics, was sitting next to Fogel; she was a woman with a loud, grating voice. "I feel terrible. A death camp. World War Two."

"Not death." Death hadn't happened yet. "Concentration."

"No wonder you have headaches." Charlotte leaned over and patted Fogel's hand.

"Don't psychoanalyze!" Fogel pushed Charlotte's hand

away. He stood up. "What do you know, psychoanalyzing? Psychoanalyze the Germans, the Poles, not the Jews. What good, to psychoanalyze the victims?"

Too loud! In Dr. Wax's office, loud could be a mistake. Dr. Wax enjoyed shouting. "Try screaming," he had once told Fogel. "Cry." This was his recommendation after Fogel's first visit, when he had stood up out of his big leather chair and escorted Fogel to the office door to indicate that the appointment-time was ended. "Who knows? Maybe crying will help." Screaming, shrieking, shouting, weeping, crying: These were Dr. Wax's cures. Also paying.

Fogel caught his breath. He sat down again. "Cancer, you know you're going to die." Now he was whispering. "So! That's it. You die. Chemicals. You spit up. Your hair falls out. So what! Already my hair fell out."

"But it grew back!" Dr. Wax smiled triumphantly.

Charlotte's hands were resting on her lap. She patted her own hand. "I thought they shaved the heads to keep the lice away."

"'Lice also. They didn't take good care of lice. In the camps lice died like flies." Fogel snickered: a historic Bergen-Belsen joke. "Two headaches, ten? A million headaches? Lice? Camps? This is not a reason for headaches. Crazy!"

"Maybe your wife is causing the headaches. Your daughter." Like a camp inmate, Charlotte did not give up easily.

Guessings! Imaginings! This was how members of the group were supposed to help each other. With explanations. Schwartz wears skirts in order to please his mother. Macy is silent in order to punish his father. Fogel refused to look in Charlotte's direction. He too did not give up easily. Proof: He was now sitting on East Seventy-ninth Street in America in the midst of a new, ersatz family.

"Are your parents still alive?"

"Smoke! They went up in smoke, puff. Pall Mall. He was the Pall, she was the Mall, a Marlboro, Kent Filter." Before, only Lillian and his children had dared to ask Fogel questions. Now there was a class. "Don't ask about my parents." Fogel sighed. He tapped his index finger against his thumb as if he were flicking cigarette ashes away. "Don't ask."

Don't ask this, don't ask that. So what if the group neurotics called Fogel a "Do-not-touch," a patient who refused to answer certain questions. So what! "No." Fogel sighed again, superbly. "Don't ask me my parents."

"What would you want to talk about, then?" Dr. Wax asked, and they all leaned forward, just a little, looking. Was he a TV set? To scandals they would listen, to revelations. If he gave his lecture on *Nathan der Weise,* they'd run away, they'd giggle, they'd yawn, they'd look at each other and make faces, they'd whisper.

"The headaches. This I can talk about."

"They must be terrible," Terry murmured. "It must feel terrible."

"It does. All the time, all day, sometimes in the library, in the subway." Fogel turned to Charlotte. "You will understand this." Charlotte refused to smile. "Sometimes like a needle in the head. Some days here." He rubbed his forehead. "Some days here." He rubbed the right temple. "Some days here." He rubbed the left temple.

But Jerusalem was besieged for months without falling. People have suffered worse things. Men have strokes; they can't move. Men go insane; they don't know where they are. Men get put into concentration camps. "I still think it's a tumor," Fogel said.

Terry smiled at him gratefully.

But Dr. Wax looked unhappy.

"I'm sorry that you had such a hard life," Charlotte said,

"but you can have a headache without being such a sour-puss." As she spoke, her own face soured with anti-Fogel sentiments. "Why are you such a sourpuss? I have head-aches too sometimes, but I don't take it out on the world."

Terry looked shocked. Annabel, the jealous wife, looked wary. Schwartz looked pleased, Macy unconcerned. Dr. Wax, on the other hand, looked interested.

"What's the matter with you, Charlotte?" Terry's voice harshened, crackling like Charlotte's own voice. "Because of the concentration camp. Wouldn't you be sour if you'd been in a concentration camp?"

"I bet he was a sourpuss before he ever even went to the concentration camp. He has a sour personality." Following the group custom, Schwartz addressed these statements to Dr. Wax, rather than to the person being discussed. "Even as a kid probably." But suddenly Schwartz switched direc-tion and aimed directly at Fogel. "Did you ever have fun? Did you ever play ball?"

Fun: a pocket full of posies, holding Marlene's little-girl hands, both hands, and dancing in a circle. Ball: kicking the helmet of the SS man, Heuser, Pisslicker Heuser, the helmet only, not the head, in Belsen the morning after liberation. The answers to Schwartz's questions: yes. The answer given: silence.

Macy made one of his rare contributions to the conver-sation. "In Europe they play soccer."

Dr. Wax, the father of this family, seemed to have no desire to control son Schwartz. Instead it was son Fogel he wished to control. "What do you think of what they've been saying?" he asked.

"What do I think?" Not a loud answer. A calm answer. "What do I think? Finished. This is what I think. Finished with yes. Finished with nice. You—" Fogel turned to Char-

52

lotte. "I don't care, you. I don't give a hoot. Two hoots. No, no, no. Not my new family. If you think this is my new family, Dr. Wax, you are deceiving yourself."

"MARLENE? MARLENE?" After consulting the telephone list posted on the refrigerator door, Fogel dialed 617-555-5978, an easy push-button number but an ordeal on a rotary dial. Fortunately Teddy didn't answer the telephone. "Marlene, do you consider you father a sourpuss?"

"Who's been calling you names?"

"In the psychotherapy group which I have been attending recently in order to cure my headaches, in this psychotherapy group, names are called, epithets. For me specifically: sourpuss."

"Why?"

"Merely because I complain about painful headaches."

"Is the doctor helping them?"

"Help. No help. What help? Headaches, a permanent headache, almost a year now. But why worry you, why bother you? This is not why I am telephoning, headaches. Sourpuss, this is the reason why."

"You're not a sourpuss. My daddy! You're a sweetie-puss, not a sourpuss." Marlene laughed, a song, four or five musical notes ascending a scale. "Cutie-pie puss, that's who you are. Right! I know that! You know what Teddy would do if somebody called him that kind of name?"

Could Fogel know the answer to this question? Did Fogel even know Teddy? A smile-puss. "I do not know the answer to this question."

"Teddy would make a joke about it. Or Teddy would find some name to call them right back."

Calling names!

Fogel himself had called names. At Marlene, many

53

names—all of them sweet: Marlinka when she was little, also Mireleh; Marloise, one rainy Saturday afternoon when he took her to tea at the Plaza after reading the book about Eloise, a girl who lived in the hotel; Marabella, when Marlene appeared at dinner one evening wearing eye make-up to prove that she was old enough to wear it; Marlinda, when she dressed in a pink gown to go to the prom with a boy.

Also at Steven, many names: Detective, when Steven wanted to play police with his father; Admiral, when he and Fogel assembled Steven's bathtub navy; Champion, when Fogel drove him to his Youth League basketball games; Champion again on the ride home if the team had won; Sport if the team had lost; and Steve when Steven was fifteen and decided to alter his name.

"Lillian," Fogel called out in the middle of the night. "Lillian!" The call would be loud enough in broad daylight; it was doubly loud at night. "Lillian!"

"What? What? Chaim, are you all right?"

Lillian's slippers scraped on the hallway floor, she was running down the stairs. Fogel was sitting at the kitchen table. "What's the matter. Are you all right?"

"I wish to tell you something." Fogel's voice was almost motionless. "I wish to tell you. From now on I wish you to do something for me."

"What?"

"Don't call me Chaim anymore. Don't use this name."

"What's the matter with you? Are you going crazy? In the middle of the night." She sat down next to him. "In a certain way going to a psychiatrist makes sense for you." She closed her eyes. "You'll be able to accept Marlene's marriage."

"I wish you to call me Fogel."

"Fogel?" Lillian sounded as if she had never heard the name before.

"My last name. My family."

"What's the matter with you?"

"My family is all dead. Gone to smoke."

"That family is dead. You have another family."

"Fogel."

She reached over and put her arms around him. He shook her away.

"Listen to me," he said. "Don't minimize." His neurotic-group members had listened to him attentively. His own family, now dead, they too had listened attentively when, once before, sitting at a table, he had resolved to abandon the name Chaim, a name that had belonged to his father's father's father.

That was in Lvov in 1941, when he was hoping to enter the university, where a Chaim was not admitted so easily. "What do you think?" he asked his parents and sister. That table was round and of dark wood. This table also was round, but it was made of white formica, manufactured from petroleum. "What do you think, Henryk?"

"Vodsic," his sister had suggested, her voice coarsening because it was a farm-boy's name. "Jacek? Ivan?" The Russians had come to Lvov; now it was a Soviet city. His father had recently grown a heavy mustache and taken up pipe smoking.

This was Fogel's family—not Terry, not Schwartz, not Charlotte. "I become the group's father in a sense," Dr. Wax had told Fogel. "That's how the therapeutic process works."

Fogel's own father tapped his pipe against the table. "Josef, this is the name.

"Pilsudski," Fogel's own father said. This meant that if the Russians ever left, Josef was a name which would not antagonize Poles. "Stalin," his father said. "Also," Fogel's mother added—they were speaking German, the language of her youth and education—"also Goebbels."

But before Fogel could go to the district office to ask if it was possible to get a new identity card, it was June; the Germans arrived. Thenceforth he was Israel, he was Abraham, he was Jew, he was Dreckiges, Arscholch, Rotzer. What names! In the camps what had he not been called: Front Hole, Back Hole, Prick, Shittypants (often, sad to say, this was true), Pisslicker (true also, after he had been ordered to clean with his tongue a floor which had been soiled by the notorious SS man Heuser); Turd, Toilet, Toilet Seat. And most terrifying: Yatkeklotz—chopping block.

Most of these were names which Fogel had also heard called out at God.

But he had not only been called evil names. Had he not also been called Elf and Rascal when he was very young and tried to tickle his father's feet? Had he not often been called Clever Youth by his father—"Isn't he clever?"—looking over reports sent back from school? Also on those days his mother had called him Clever Boy in the apartment overlooking the tramline, the one they had lived in before the Soviet army came. "An outstanding student." Had he not been called this by Professor Robinson of Columbia University when he was getting his Ph.D.?

Also Darling. Was he not called Darling by Lillian when they were first married, until together they decided this was a foolish way to talk. Maybe in Hollywood people talked so, maybe now Steven was accustomed to breathe this word into the ear of a starlet, but it was not the way people talked in the Bronx on Walton Avenue. He had been called Sweetheart

56

by the prostitute on Eighth Avenue the week before he was married, Puppy by the prostitute in Hamburg, Big Man by the Polish woman in Hannover.

And now Sourpuss!

"No more Chaim!" Fogel hit the table with the palm of his hand. "No more Chaim. Listen to me. My father is dead. My mother."

"I think psychiatry is getting you overwrought." Lillian took Fogel's hand, the one that hadn't slapped the table, and held it. "Why did you come downstairs?"

"Eat."

"What did you eat?"

"Cornflakes."

"Have we got enough milk for coffee in the morning?" Lillian leaned forward and inspected Fogel's empty cereal bowl.

"I'll have tea."

"No, I'll have tea. If there's any milk left, you have it with coffee."

"What does it matter?" Fogel's hand slipped away. "I eat anything. Tea, coffee, I'm thankful."

"Chaim, don't talk like that. Every day you have coffee. If you want coffee, drink coffee."

"Just Fogel. Not Chaim, just Fogel."

VI

I feel so bad I didn't know about Bergman-Belsen," Terry whispered. This week Fogel made sure he was sitting next to Terry, not Charlotte.

Fogel whispered too: "Not Bergman, Bergen. Bergman is cinema."

"I didn't even pronounce it right. Bergen. That makes me feel even worse."

I feel terrible. Now I feel worse. This I feel. That I feel. Feel! Feel!—every week in Dr. Wax's psychotherapeutic group. Europeans know about "I feel!" Survivors know: Less is better. But Terry, Charlotte, every one of them: I feel! Also the men, also Schwartz. In Dr. Wax's office, feelings flourish like jungle trees. "I feel ashamed," Schwartz has said. His skin, except for the freckles, turns pink, a brassiere color. "I can't help it. I feel this need. Silk." Schwartz hangs his head down. He looks at nobody. "I get overwhelmed with feelings about panties. Then I feel horny." Charlotte also feels. "I feel anxious. I feel so anxious now." Her hands become white. Her face becomes pale. From feeling Schwartz pinks. Charlotte, on the other hand, whitens. Annabel, the jealous wife, also changes color as a result of feeling: red. Tears shine on her cheeks. "I feel he doesn't love me." Her

58

voice chokes. "I always feel nobody loves me." She reaches for a tissue from the box beside Dr. Wax's chair and blows her nose. "Only my grandmother. I feel she's the only one who ever loved me."

Too much feeling! And Marlene also. Is not excessive feeling the cause of Fogel's headaches? Although when Fogel sat down beside Terry, his headache began to flutter, perhaps preparing to fly away back to the treasury where God keeps headaches stored.

"I feel terrible." Terry reached out her hand toward Fogel, a gesture merely. Her hand didn't actually touch him. Still, from this almost touch, Fogel's head pain altered, becoming an almost headache. "It isn't like I didn't know about the concentration camps. My father has this book about them. Whenever I wanted to cry, I used to take the book and hold it on my lap and then I'd cry."

Remembering her tears, Terry saddened. Similarly, Fogel saddened: His headache returned.

"Why'd you want to cry?" Schwartz asked before Fogel had the opportunity to inquire himself.

"You know, like when people want to cry. Everybody wants to cry, right?"

"Right," Dr. Wax declared. Nobody contradicted him.

Did Fogel want to cry? No. Why should Fogel now cry? Let God cry.

"You should have come to me whenever you felt like crying." Schwartz smiled at Terry, as if this offer would certainly make her happy. "I would have made you feel a lot better."

"No way!" Terry said. She turned toward Fogel. "That's why I do this deep breathing now." She inhaled, but lightly this time. "I wish I could do something to, like, make you feel better. Anything."

"Anything?" Fogel asked boldly. Should Schwartz think he is the only macho in the room?

Charlotte giggled. Perhaps now Fogel was no longer a sourpuss to her. Terry only said, "Ha-ha."

"Ha-ha." This is what she said. Not "Drop dead!" Not "Buzz off!" Merely "Ha-ha." A "Ha-ha" is not a "No." It is not a "Never." Perhaps it is even a "Maybe."

Maybe. Who knows? Anything could happen. Indeed, as Fogel stood before his class the next day lecturing—"The American Revolution did not occur in a vacuum. There are statues of George Washington. Also there should be statues of Voltaire and Diderot. Thanks to the men of the Enlightenment we have freedom of religion"—the classroom door noisily opened and in walked Terry. She sat down in the back row, next to a hippie-looking student wearing a motorcycle jacket. Hippie smiled at her. Also a blue-jeans boy winked at her. Also, a horn-rims spectacles turned around and stared.

"Attacking established religion was one of the most significant programs of the Enlightenment." Just as if Terry had not walked into the classroom, startlingly interrupting his carefully written Voltaire-eulogy, Fogel continued. "This is the program: to destroy the power of religion over the people." Piously his students took notes. "Wipe out the infamy! This is what Voltaire declared." One girl in the front row was not writing. She was twirling a lock of hair around her finger. "Write this down in your notebook," Fogel sternly commanded her. "Write it down. Wipe out the infamy!" The girl wrote.

As soon as Fogel had finished his lecture, Terry ran up to him at the lectern, past blue-jeans and horn-rims, past hippie, though hippie was a sexy with a leather jacket, a devil-may-care. "Come with me. I know how to get rid of your headaches. Pauline. My friend Pauline. She's fabulous. She'll know what to do."

"Don't be nervous," Terry whispered as they walked into Pauline's apartment building. "I told her what's wrong. She might do aura. She might do white magic."

Terry looked like a girl horn-rims might escort, or Mr. Hippie Leather Jacket; yet it was Professor Fogel's arm she was holding as she walked through the apartment lobby. In every man's life there are unexpected occurrences. The more enlightened he is, the more sophisticated and tolerant is his manner of greeting them. Why not aura to cure headaches? Why not white magic? Who can tell where science will lead mankind? Why couldn't it be a lucky sign that the elevator man took them to the seventh floor? "I feel foolish," Fogel said. "I feel ludicrous. White magic."

Terry laughed. "Don't be silly," she said.

Pauline was a tall, pale-eyed woman with a fluty voice. She was wearing dangling earrings and a long white dress. Her apartment had a view of Washington Square. It had a grandfather clock, it had an embroidered footstool, it had a china cupboard displaying a collection of porcelain birds, owls—some little, some big. On the sofa there were comic books. Here children lived. Was this a witch? The witch woman of Drohobych had stood in front of the oil wellhead every day as the work-camp Jews were marched by, an old Ukrainian woman wearing German soldier boots and a balding fur coat. Even in winter she held fresh grass in her hand. "Seventy-two," she would whisper hoarsely, never looking the Jews in the eye. "Seventy-two! Anael. I make you a life charm."

To her Fogel had said no. But now it was yes.

Pauline's children were still at school. "The Little Red Schoolhouse here in the Village. Do you know it?" Pauline leaned her head forward and her shoulders too, as if she would gobble Fogel up. Her eyes turned dark, like blood.

"Private?" Fogel said bravely. "A private school?"

"Let's get going." Pauline hurried into the dining room. "My cleaning woman's coming soon." The dining room had a big Oriental rug on the floor. "Come on." She motioned to Fogel to sit down at the head of the dining table.

Terry followed them into the room. "You, you go back there." Pauline waved her hand toward the living room. "You look out the window. Look at the view."

Pauline sat down next to Fogel. "Put your hands over your eyes."

Fogel did as he was told. But shouldn't he also see the mystery? He peeked.

"Don't look." Pauline spoke sternly. "You're nervous. You don't need to be nervous." Her voice softened. "You don't need to worry."

Fogel's fingers closed. The High Priest of the Temple in Jerusalem had opened his fingers wide whenever he blessed the people in order to let the spirit of God rush through. Fogel opened his fingers just a crack. Had his head stopped hurting already? No. A little bit? No. Nevertheless, certainly it would be impolite for an enlightened man, visiting a fine apartment, to inform the kind hostess who was endeavoring to help him that her efforts were ineffective, indeed foolish, indeed crazy.

In Fogel's grandfather's village there had also been a witch. "Hell! Hell!" his grandfather said whenever they walked by her little wooden house. He always held on to Fogel's hand tightly.

The first time this happened Fogel began to cry. "Hell! Hell! Why hell, hell, zayde?" Although he was very young, although he was crying, he knew enough to talk to this grandfather in Yiddish, not in German.

"A witch. A spellmaker. Even a Jew! Even a Jew!" But Fogel and his grandfather were on the way to the prayer house, so it didn't matter.

That witch didn't stop the German army.

Pauline sat down opposite Fogel. She took off her earrings and placed them neatly on either side of a little bowl that stood on the table in front of her. Fogel could see! Then, slowly and delicately, she poured something—was it milk?— from a little pitcher into the bowl. While she poured, she hummed—one long low note. When she finished, she shut her eyes and put the flat of her hand on her forehead. Her lips moved. A bone-china sugar bowl and cream pitcher, decorated with blue flowers. This Lillian would love.

"Open your eyes."

Fogel put his hands on the table.

"Good," Pauline said loudly.

"What good?" Fogel still had his headache. Not a knife-headache as in the morning, not a many-needles, but the worst kind, a gouger.

"Now your headaches will go away." Terry took Fogel's arm as they walked together through the park, returning to the campus. They will go away. They will go away. Maybe Terry was correct. Suddenly, for a moment, instead of the gouger, something else came to visit Fogel's head: dizziness. "Uh!" Fogel pulled his arm away. "Uh! Maybe Pauline's magic is working."

"Whoopee!" Terry yelled. "Whoopee!" She turned to face Fogel and stood on tiptoe to hold on to his ears and kiss him on the forehead—even in front of the black men sitting, unemployed, on the park benches, even in front of any students who might be passing by. Never mind students. In front of faculty!

"Uh!" Fogel said again. "Uh!" With Terry's kiss, the gouger returned: a punishment from hell. Again headache. As if magic, foolishness, superstition, as if Terry-comfort could really cure headaches!

"Wait! The process is just beginning." This was Terry's promise. And indeed on the train home the gouger departed, at the Tuckahoe stop.

"WHOOPEE! Again today: no headache." Fogel walked into the kitchen where the Friday chicken was cooking. He clapped his hands. "Whoopee!" Was there not reason to applaud? "Thursday, also Friday—no headaches. Whoopee! Again I say it. Whoopee, hurrah, wonderful!"

"Wonderful is right!" Lillian lowered the flame under the chicken pot. "I can see a real difference in you. Dr. Wax's therapy is working."

"Dr. Wax's therapy is working." With these very words, on that very afternoon, Lillian had comforted Marlene, who telephoned from Boston. "I'm worried about Daddy," Marlene had said. "Someone called him a sourpuss and he got so upset about it he had to call me up for reassurance. It was scary."

"You don't have to worry. Daddy's OK. He's a lot better. People start with a psychiatrist, they go through a lot of turmoil. It's part of the process. He's getting better. I see little signs. You know, yesterday he came up to me, he put his arms around me, he kissed me for no reason at all, just like a newlywed. So don't you worry about Daddy."

"Dr. Wax is working wonders for you, Chaim." Lillian lifted the pot lid to inspect the chicken. "What's his secret?

64

Don't tell me. I don't want to know. It's your business, between you and the psychiatrist. I don't need to know."

Chicken, onion, carrots, celery: The sweet savor made Fogel rejoice. Fogel, Chaim, Fogel. Does a name matter? No, what matters is a head without pain! What matters is a tongue tasting food! "How soon dinner? Six o'clock? Seven?"

"Six. Always six."

"I want candles." Fogel leaned over the stove and sniffed. "I want wine. I want bread. Make sure you cover the bread with a nice napkin."

Could this be another way to cure headaches? Insurance, just in case Terry's witch-magic stops working? So it might be considered if Fogel were a superstitious man. But Fogel is a man who has devoted his life to the study of the Enlightenment. Even though he is a man who suffers from headaches, a man subject now to teeth grinding, to eye shuts, a man who may be dying, what are candles to him, what are bread and wine for welcoming the Sabbath? Merely an excursion into nostalgia, merely pretty gestures, merely a reminder of certain pleasant childhood memories.

"It's silly, only the two of us. When the children were here, we never did it." Nevertheless, Lillian set the table exactly the right way. "I feel like I'm back in my mother's house."

Fogel stood up and read the prayer. He sang the blessing. He drank the wine. He cut the bread and handed a piece to his wife. He made a joke: "For dinner tonight, what? Peanut soup?" But as he read the prayer, the back of his head started hurting again.

"Welcome the bride," Lillian said when she brought a bowl of chicken soup out to the dining-room table. Even

Fogel's father, the socialist ideologue, had loved Jewish chicken soup. But when Fogel put the hot spoon to his mouth, his lips felt numb, as if from Novocain; but he hadn't been to the dentist.

"Sing the songs now." Even after dessert was finished Lillian remained seated. "They were always so pretty."

But Fogel couldn't sing them. These customs had never been performed in his house, only in the houses of his grandparents, his friends. True, he had heard his grandfather singing after meals: "I have been young; now I am old. I have not seen the righteous abandoned." In the camps he had heard men sing after eating food: "He shall rule over us forever." But he himself didn't know these songs. For he had been raised in the house of a rationalist. "Hitler rules Germany," his father had said more than once. "Stalin rules Russia. But the numbers one, two, five and zero rule the universe." He would take Fogel's hand into his own and declare: "Before the numbers one, two, five and zero, even the czar had to bow down."

Should Fogel now count himself among irrational men by becoming a singer of psalms? One more irrational man? In his lifetime he had seen too many irrational men, and not only the anti-Semites. In the camps some men were so irrational that they played mystical games with the numbers tattooed on their arms. This was their lowly pleasure. One man insisted that his number, in its Hebrew letter equivalents, spelled out the word Messiah. A second declared that his number was an acronym: its letter equivalents began certain lines of the psalm: God to whom vengeance belongs, God to whom vengeance belongs, shine forth. A third claimed that he wore on his arm in numbers the verse: "The adversary and enemy is this wicked Haman." A fourth sifted numbers and letters until he came up with the verse: "I shall execute judgment on you in anger and in fury." These men were dead. Fogel was alive, and without having depended on prayers.

Once at Auschwitz, one of the irrational men had grasped his hand to inspect his number: 866427. The Hebrew letters for it were Ches, Vov, Vov, Daled, Bes, Zayin. "They could make many holy words. They could be read in many ways: 86–6427; 866–427." Fogel had snatched his arm away. "The permutations are endless. A mathematician would know them," he said with contempt. "This is God's joke."

But while Lillian was washing the dishes after dinner, Fogel went upstairs to Steven's neat, unused room and sat down on the green bedspread to browse through the Hebrew Bible, one of his son's Bar Mitzvah gifts. Ches, Vov, Vov, Daled, Bes, Zayin. These were not the letters of "the righteous perishes"; but on the other hand neither were they the letters of "Fear not, O Jacob, my servant." Fogel put the book down on the floor. No! Immediately, he picked it up— it was the Bible. Though an enlightened man should not have such superstitions, he gently set it on Steven's bed.

1489A. 1489B. These were the numbers of the cemetery plots where Fogel and Lillian would one day lie. Numbers, needles. Again: a many-needles. Again, a killer.

Fogel went to bed.

"CHAIM, WAKE UP!" Lillian came into the bedroom carrying coffee and coffee cake. "Fresh-baked. Fresh-brewed. A lovely day. No classes. Let's just go for a ride."

Fogel was already awake. "To the graveyard. This is where I'll ride."

Lillian tried to pull the covers off. "I'm tired of these jokes," she said. "This depression."

"I am not joking." Fogel held on to the blanket and rolled

over to lie on his back, face up: corpse position. "I will ride only to Long Island."

Is this an appropriate way to respond to a woman who brings her husband breakfast in bed? Is this the act of a gallant man? "You are so gallant, monsieur!" Lillian said every year on her birthday when Fogel carried in her breakfast tray. And when she carried in his tray on his birthday she always said, "You deserve this, monsieur, because you have been such a brave man."

Brave, who cares brave now? Gallant, what matter? Why pretend brave? Headache brave? Dying brave? What good brave? Let Lillian be brave. Let Marlene, let Pauline. Let Teddy, let Terry. Finished, brave. Forget it, brave. "Only to the cemetery. This is what I wish to see."

"We've already seen it." Lillian backed away from the bed. "We went when we bought. Then we went back for my cousin Murray's funeral."

"I want to go again."

"How's your head?"

"My head. My head. That's how it is."

"I won't go. It's morbid. We'll be spending plenty of time there. Why rush?"

But she went.

"My husband is never cheerful anymore since our daughter married a man of another background," Lillian had written to the famous Dr. Koppel, who provided advice to the suffering in a newspaper column. Fogel had even seen the letter while he was reading the afternoon paper one day on the train home to White Plains. So? In his lifetime, a man reads many such letters. "My husband is a man who has had a very hard life," the letter said. "He was never very cheerful to begin with. Now all he does is complain, mostly about physical symptoms, although the doctors say there is

68

nothing wrong with him. Not just one doctor says this. We've consulted two. We have a second opinion from a psychiatrist. Most of the time our sex life is a disaster area. I am a very optimistic and lighthearted woman, on the other hand. I try to be warmhearted and accept my son-in-law just as I accept my husband's peculiarities. (He is foreign born.) But now I am at my wit's end. Though I try to cater to my husband, nothing I do seems to make any difference."

Dr. Koppel's answer, kept hidden in the secret compartment of Lillian's jewelry chest, was chilling. If Fogel, like Schwartz in the psychotherapy group, had the habit of rummaging through his wife's jewelry chest, he would have come across it. It suggested an unnatural attachment between Fogel and Marlene. It warned that loss in middle age or older—the loss of a job, the marriage of a beloved child—could lead to irreversible depression, shock treatment, suicide. "Keep busy," Dr. Koppel advised. "Try to distract and occupy the depressed person. But if the depression continues, it is advisable to seek further professional help."

"Where is mine," Fogel demanded when they got to the cemetery, "1489A? 1489B?"

Lillian walked along, following signs. "It's not so pretty this time," she said mournfully. "This is morbid. Why are you so morbid? Just from headaches? From Marlene?" Plastic numbers on little sticks marked each plot. Lillian reached 1489A. "In the summer it will be pretty." She lightly touched the stick.

The plots were in a section of the cemetery which only recently had been unpopulated. Now stones were going up here and there: 1485A and B, 1491, 1485B.

"When I die," Fogel said fiercely, "I want you to plant a tree." He knelt down and patted the turf at the head of 1489A. "Right here."

"You don't plant in the cemetery. It's against the rules." Lillian shivered. "You plant trees in Israel, not in the cemetery."

"For me a tree." Fogel stood up again; he leaned over; he bent his head forward; he spit, down at the spot where one day his skull would lie. "There!" He spit again. "This is a little souvenir for God. There! There is where I want a tree."

"You are too angry about Marlene." Lillian took his arm. "Marlene is driving you crazy. She is making love in bed with Teddy. So you won't make love yourself."

Fogel covered his face with his hands.

"Two minutes!" Lillian sang out. "Two minutes and we're out of here. We'll drive to Long Beach to look at some new condominiums I saw advertised. Just to look. They sound lovely."

Fogel didn't move.

"Chaim?" Lillian said.

Still Fogel didn't move.

"Traffic." Lillian was smiling. "The slower we move the worse the traffic gets." She took Fogel's arm and began to steer him out of the graveyard. "Chaim, let's get going. I'll start the car."

"Condominiums, never mind," Fogel said while he was buckling his safety belt. He was allowing Lillian to drive. "1489A. That's my condominium: 1489A."

VII

N
ever mind!" Fogel said to Steven over the telephone. It was another one of his late-night calls. "It's all right, go with your Hindus, your Hare Krishnas. Even Lessing at the end of his life became a pantheist. If him, why not you? If you, why not me?"

Why not? Why not a new religious cult, psychotherapy? Why not witches? "Why not pantheism? Is there a God?"

"Christ, I'm not a Hindu!" Was Steven's sourpuss voice merely an echo of Fogel's? "That stuff doesn't mean anything to me. Jesus, how do I know if there's a God!" Or was this Steven's own voice, inherited? "You should know. You're the professor, not me."

Is this honoring a Jewish father, commandment number five, addressing him so, impatiently and with frequent Christian references?

"All I'm doing is watching the Krishnas. Cinematically. You know, shooting. It's just a cult. Like the Moonies. Jesus! Like the Jews too, for that matter. Why do you keep hassling me about it?"

Technically the message is going through, up to the satellite in heaven, over the trees, over the dead in the earth, over the Jews, over the anti-Semites. But is the message being received? Fogel sat, hardly listening, twisting the tele-

71

phone cord. "Hindus, Buddhists, pagans, pantheists—all the same." He sighed, an enormous transcontinental sigh. "This is America, modern times, the children, they turn."

"Did your headaches go away?"

The answer: "Hah!"

"I heard about a new kind of photography. You can film headaches. Next time I come east I'll check out your head with it."

"A CAT scan. This I already had."

"No, Kirlian photography. It's not like a CAT scan. It gets the aura. Everybody's got an aura, like a halo, right? You'll be a pioneer with it. It's so new, you'll be a part of cinema history."

"Try it. Try it." Fogel's voice cracked. Already Fogel was part of real history; now he would be part of cinema history. "Make a movie out of me." A film spectacular: *Inside Fogel.* "Don't you worry, Steven. You shouldn't worry. Now I hang up. Be a good boy. You enjoy." As if a father had to remind a son such as Steven to enjoy, a son who insisted on going to film school in California, even though there was an outstanding film-studies program at New York University, where his father was a respected professor and where tuition therefore cost almost nothing; a son who had stated: "I have to go to the Coast. I can't shoot on my own here with you looking over my shoulder."

"You take care now," Steven said.

"Never mind me. *You* take care. Good-bye. Enjoy for me." Fogel put his hand on the telephone, he cut the connection. But for a minute longer he held the receiver to his ear. "Enjoy," he said firmly. "You enjoy." He hung up the phone. But then, suddenly, he lifted it again and pressed it against his arm. Let his body listen! Let the telephone act as a cup! Let it draw blood pressure away from the forehead! Also pain! He pushed down hard. "Enjoy," he whispered, as if Steven could still hear him. He pushed. He pushed. But the blood continued to beat at his forehead. The telephone refused to work as a cup. Fogel pressed the phone against his neck. On the neck too, ineffective. Fogel's body was not listening.

But I am listening. I hear the flesh shrieking. I hear its agonies.

"How ARE you feeling?" When Dr. Wax made this inquiry, Fogel was sitting in the group-circle again.

Fogel tapped his forehead. "Maybe I deserve headaches." A driller was arriving.

"Chaim!" Charlotte shook her head so vigorously that her earrings shook too. "Don't go on a guilt-trip. I know. I've been on plenty of them."

For Charlotte, guilt-trips, yes; subway-trips, no.

"Maybe I am a bad father. Maybe headaches attack because I am not nice to my daughter, instead of because vice versa." Fogel twisted in his chair. "Also my son accuses me of hassling."

Dr. Wax smiled—a happy smile, not just a business smile. "Then that means your headaches are psychosomatic."

"Being a bad father ..." Maybe this time it would be only a little driller. "Could this cause headaches?"

Dr. Wax answered promptly. "It's worth examining." Then, less promptly, he said, "I think you're nice."

From across the room, Terry waved at Fogel. "I think you're nice too," she called out.

Fogel smiled at Terry. "I am no sourpuss. Certainly not." Generously, he smiled at Charlotte too. Today Charlotte's hair looked stiffer than usual, almost lacquered. "Maybe sometimes a little sourpussness collects. Maybe it rushes to the head and thus I am in pain. This could be. But I have

73

often been complimented by students for wittiness." He smiled at Schwartz. Now Fogel was a smile-puss. Perhaps smiling cures headaches. TV talk shows say smiling and laughter will cure any illness. Fogel turned toward plump Annabel and smiled at her too. Macy, never mind. Finally he smiled at Dr. Wax. "Usually I think positively, with humor, thus ridding myself of troubles, why not!" Dr. Wax did not smile back. "But for headaches, no soap."

"The question is . . ." Before continuing, Dr. Wax waited until Fogel was looking at him. "Do you think you're nice?"

"Of course I am nice. You have recently heard testimony." Fogel turned his head to smile again at Terry. Then, courteously, he turned to face Dr. Wax again, even though head-moving was painful. "Among my NYU colleagues, I have many, many friends." Had Fogel ever made trouble at departmental meetings? Had Fogel ever fussed about granting tenure? "Plus, I am considered extremely nice by certain students." Hadn't Fogel written many fine, effective recommendations? "But still I suffer."

Dr. Wax gave Fogel one of his sympathy smiles. "I'm afraid you're suffering unnecessarily," he said.

"Is he the only one suffering?" Charlotte's eyes were glittering. Was it with tears?

Suffering and tears. These were the sacrifices Dr. Wax's devotees offered to him every week. In Dr. Wax's office tears flowed plentifully, Fogel had seen—not the way tears had flowed in the camps, like wine at a party, but plentifully nevertheless. Emotions! This was what Dr. Wax's neurotics offered to him, tears-and-suffering emotions: Sadness, fear, worry, anxiety, shame. Negative emotions, to use Dr. Wax's words. I can't start! I can't stop! I'm afraid. It makes me want to cry! During one group meeting Annabel, a woman sadly overweight and careless about her hair, had wept so pathetically because her husband was maintaining a mistress that Dr. Wax had handed her a tissue. Schwartz himself had cried once. Why? Because fate had made him a transvestite. "I'm so ashamed of myself." Tears made Schwartz's cheeks turn even pinker. "And now I'm crying like a girl. That makes me feel even more ashamed."

Fogel was no weeper. He would never cry again. Smiling, laughter, cheerfulness—these would help his cure. Yet on the day when Schwartz was crying, Fogel almost remembered the location of the tear-storage cave in his own head. He could almost feel it. Where? At the temple-headache place? Behind the eyebrows-headache place? Where? It scampered from one hiding place to another like a frightened Jew. Schwartz stopped crying. He took a tissue and rubbed it against his eyes. Then he blew his nose. Poor Schwartz!

"To me suffering is nothing new." Fogel sat up in his chair. He straightened his shoulders. Ranged around the room, the group sat listening. "Then I suffered, Nazis. Now I suffer, headaches. Both the same. Death-traps."

Dr. Wax shook his head from side to side. "You are trapping yourself when you think about headaches. Think about what might be causing them instead."

"Think?" This was not a little driller, a smiling matter; it was a big driller. "I have a sufficiency of insights, a professor."

A sorrow-look froze over Dr. Wax's face. "You are your own worst enemy." He sighed. Apparently, Fogel had wearied him. The group understood. Schwartz looked down toward the floor. Macy's eyes became even blanker. Annabel bit her lip. Charlotte changed the subject.

"I know the Holocaust was awful. Horrible." Charlotte's posture tightened. "But was it always so terrible in the camps? Didn't they even put on operas in some concentration camps? *Carmen?* Once I saw that on TV."

"Always terrible." Fogel's headache suddenly disappeared. Perhaps smiling had expelled it. "No opera."

"Pardon me. I didn't mean to imply anything." Charlotte began twisting one of the rings on her finger. She always wore a diamond, plus a gold ring, plain. Today also she had on a big lemon-colored stone. "I'm sorry. What work did you do there? Bodies?"

"Different places I did different things." Fogel folded his arms. "Drohobych, the work camp, I did signs. A painter. 'Hats off!' the guards would say. 'Hats on! Hats off! Down! Up! Attention! Jump! If they said it, I did it." When Steven had asked, "What did you do in the camps?" Lillian said, "Sh, don't bother him."

"Auschwitz, I carried rocks. Here to there. There to here." For a moment Fogel sat breathing heavily, as if he were still tired from lifting. "After that Belsen, sometimes bodies, dragging to the pits; sometimes no work, when they wanted to leave bodies on the ground. Belsen, I waited. I looked out." Also whenever Marlene had asked, Lillian had told her, "Never mind. Don't bother him."

Don't bother. Finished.

Suddenly, Fogel made a whistling sound. He raised his hands abruptly and covered his ears. "I don't want to talk about this. No more. Now we should shut up. They keep saying liberated, we were liberated, when we were liberated. A laugh. They are still there." Dr. Wax was watching him. Schwartz, Charlotte, Terry—all of them were staring at him. Should this make him stop? No, it should not make him stop. He would say what he thought—not what he felt, what he thought. "Now let us talk about the brave Israeli soldiers." Fogel snapped his fingers at Dr. Wax. Again he snapped, this time at Schwartz. "Jewish victories. Always the Nazis, they talk about. My son-in-law, they suffered too. The slaves, the Middle Passage? They also suffered. Talk about them."

"Your son-in-law is a Negro?" Charlotte said. She had forgotten the details of Fogel's biography.

"I thought he was a professor." Schwartz sounded shocked. He too had forgotten. All the lingerie-clutter in his mind left no room for it.

"Can't you be a black professor?" Terry said indignantly.

"A black professor. I am a white professor. She married a man like her father. She married who she wanted to marry, it's up to her. Is it up to you?" Fogel made a fist so Schwartz could see it. Also Schwartz could see this: Fogel is a gentleman, a man who refrains from shaking his fist at a fellow neurotic, but not a weak man, a womanish man. No, on the contrary, a determined man, a survivor, a man with a fierce voice. "He gets job offers, sociology, University of Maine, Queens College. Also in the South, Maryland. But he is staying in Boston. Boston University. It's like NYU there."

"That's wonderful!" Charlotte seemed to sound enthusiastic. "That's wonderful! Do they have any children?"

"Not yet!" An answer, a plea, a bargain, a prayer, a demand, a shout, a headache.

"DON'T YOU want a new baby?" Terry asked Fogel as they walked out of Dr. Wax's office. "Don't you want your daughter to enjoy herself? Don't you love your daughter?"

"Certainly I love my daughter. Of course I love my daughter." This answer was true. Also it vigorously affirmed friendship for Terry, herself a daughter.

"Take this. It's for you." Terry reached into her jacket pocket and handed Fogel a small pink envelope. On the envelope in dainty letters were written the words: "Professor

Fogel. Do not open." "I told Pauline you were still having your headaches. Pauline said to take this envelope and burn it in your hearth."

"I do not have a hearth." Fogel held the envelope with his fingertips. "But thank you for your thoughtfulness. Also thank your friend Pauline." Fogel smiled at Terry, a broad smile such as the smile he used to smile at Lillian when he was younger. "Thoughtfulness. Helpfulness." Of all the group members—this included Dr. Wax—Terry was the most eager to help. "Helpfulness. Kindness. I have noticed that these are qualities in Dr. Wax's group."

Was Fogel telling lies merely to ingratiate himself with Terry, a bad student, but an original and attractive girl, a simpatico girl—no, simpatica as the Spanish might say; indeed a girl who looked a little Spanish, not Puerto Rican, certainly not, but Spanish: Seville, perhaps, Toledo, once a great center of Jewish culture. Was Fogel telling lies? Certainly not. The truth was the truth.

Helpfulness. Even Schwartz. Often, after group meetings, Schwartz kindly drove his fellow neurotics to their destinations—Charlotte to West Eighty-sixth Street, Macy to his bus station, Fogel to Grand Central, Terry downtown to her friend's loft—before he himself traveled home to Cedarhurst on Long Island. Helpfulness: Had not Charlotte offered to assist Fogel in purchasing a new diamond ring for Lillian so that his sex life would improve and his headaches disappear? Helpfulness. Thus was it not appropriate to respond with pleasant smiles to Dr. Wax's psychotherapeutic group?

"A hearth is a fireplace." Terry gave a helpful answer. "Do you have a fireplace?"

"We don't use our fireplace."

"Follow instructions exactly, Pauline said." In the group a certain tone of voice was employed when a member was

78

"resisting" any counsel that was being offered. Now Terry was using this voice. "Exactly."

"Hearth. Can this also mean furnace?" Fogel inspected the envelope as if it could answer his question. Resisting psychotherapy, so what! Resisting irresistible Terry. Could Fogel do this?

Impatiently, Terry raked her fingers through her hair. "You're the professor."

A professor who has succumbed to witchery. An enlightened man, a Ph.D.

Witchery. Psychiatry. So what, one more superstition. Formerly, enlightened men refused to believe the camps could exist. Now doctors refused to believe in brain tumors. Instead they believed in psychiatry. "You are in charge of your own head," Dr. Wax had said. "Nobody else. Only you." About this Dr. Wax was in error. About this, no smiling. God was in charge of Fogel's head—that is, if there was a God. And now God was finished with Fogel. God was erasing the name Chaim Fogel from the Book of Life. So what! Big deal! Fogel was also finished with God. Let God put that in his pipe and smoke it. Because certainly God had given Fogel a brain tumor. Certainly the doctors had made a mistake interpreting Fogel's CAT scan. Therefore Fogel would obey the instructions of a witch. Therefore Fogel would become a pagan, like Steven's Hare Krishnas, like Marlene's Africans.

"No!" Lillian shrieked when she saw Fogel on his knees in front of the fireplace. "No!" The decorative brass fan that usually sat in the fireplace was folded up on the living-room floor. In its place was a pile of crumpled newspapers ready to be lit, and on top of them a clean birch log, one of three which had been sitting for ten years beside the fireplace in a shining brass bin. "So white!" Lillian had always rejoiced at the paint inside the fireplace. "So clean!" When

Marlene had requested a fire in honor of her sweet-sixteen party, Lillian had said, "No, it's a shame to dirty it. You're pure, let it be pure. A symbol."

"What are you doing?" Lillian shouted at Fogel. "Stop it! No!"

"Chilly," Fogel mumbled. The envelope was in his shirt pocket. "A fire. I thought a fire."

Lillian took the matches out of his hand as if he were a child. She picked up the log and carefully restored it to its place in the bin. "You clean up the newspapers," she commanded. "I do enough cleaning." This was true; at times Fogel had seen her dusting the logs. "Sometimes your behavior!" she said impatiently. "Who can blame you after the camps? But sometimes your behavior!" As she hurried out of the room, she called back: "No discussions! Discuss it with your Dr. Wax."

Downstairs in the cellar, a devilish fire burned inside the furnace. Carefully, Fogel took the envelope out of his pocket, brushed it against his lips and waved it gently back and forth in front of the flame. He had opened the furnace door boldly without wearing gloves. Now he got as close to the fire as he dared. "Go!" he whispered. "Go!" He let the envelope drop into the flames. It flared. A sweet smell came out of the fire.

Where was the message going? Certainly not to Jerusalem, to the hearth of the Jews' God. Because while Fogel was climbing back up the cellar stairs, holding onto the rail carefully—he felt weak, he felt dizzy—the telephone was ringing.

It was Marlene calling from Boston with good news again: She was pregnant.

VIII

C ome." Lillian squeezed the upper part of Fogel's arm, at the place where the muscle had been hardened by camp stone-lifting. "We're going to temple tonight. Purim."

"Is this the proper environment for a husband with headaches? Noisemakers?"

"You complain when it's quiet too. What difference does it make?"

"Always moving! Always going out! A headache. Do you think all the noisiness will help?"

Cursed be Haman! It is Fogel who is cursed.

Only once had Fogel heard a quiet celebration of Purim, in the Drohobych work-camp. There none of the Jews dared make enough noise to kill the name of Haman when the scroll of Esther was being read. There the Jews dared only to hiss quietly when they heard the villain's name; or they sighed loudly, as if to approximate a hiss. And in the other camps, there was never a scroll to be read.

But everywhere else, Purim had to be celebrated with noise. In Lvov the Jews paraded back and forth in the streets singing and calling out, "Cursed! Cursed! *Arur Haman!*" Only in the Jewish streets, of course. His mother always drew the curtains closed. "I want to go out," Fogel said the year he was fifteen. With a fist, his father pointed to Fogel's room. "Go study. This will curse Haman." But Fogel disobeyed. He ran through the dark, noisy streets looking for his friends. At this time they called each other by Polish names. Fogel was Henryk. In front of the dairy-food shop, he found his friend Simcha, known as Stasio, the Simcha who died in the Jankowska camp, not the Simcha who disappeared from Lvov after the Soviet army came. "Cursed be Haman," they shouted together. Simcha-Stasio had a small flask of brandy. They drank it and Fogel flirted with a busty girl who refused to tell him her name. "I am Queen Esther," she insisted. Fogel steered her into a doorway and kissed her. It was the only time he ever became drunk. The Jews are saved, Hitler will be destroyed, Haman is dead, the Romans are gone, the Assyrians are gone. Where are the Babylonians now?

"Near the back! Near the back!" Cautiously, Fogel walked behind Lillian into the big, wood-paneled White Plains temple. "In case we have to leave." He waved his hand in front of his forehead. The room was crowded and as noisy as the streets of Lvov. "Beautiful!" Lillian pointed to the brightly lighted candelabrum, a work of modern sculpture, hammered brass, twisted and tortured like a Jew. "Isn't that beautiful!" Fogel followed her into a pew. On either side of them sat young children, squirming.

"Look!" Again Lillian squeezed Fogel's arm. "Look!" There, sitting two rows in front of them, was a black child, a boy of about eight, smooth-skinned, not exactly black but the color of parchment—astonishingly, the color of a Torah-scroll. Like all the other children he sat wriggling excitedly, listening to the Hebrew recitation, waiting for the one word he could understand, the word Haman. Whenever he heard it, he jumped up along with all the other children and enthusiastically whirled his noisemaker. Cursed be Haman! Cursed! With her knuckle, Lillian nudged Fogel in the ribs.

"A Jewish child! He could be Marlene's."

A boy still too small to have a history, yet a boy with two faces. He was sitting between two white parents.

"Maybe adopted," Fogel said.

"Maybe from an earlier marriage. An intermarriage."

Before Fogel could answer, the word Haman was read again. Fogel whirled the noisemaker in his hand. He stamped his feet. He roared. Although he was looking above the head of the mixling-child, at the reader on the platform, he could see Lillian watching him.

"See!" As soon as it was quiet again, Lillian put her hand on his arm, this time directly over the numbers hidden under the sleeve of his jacket. "They could raise their children as Jews. It goes by the mother. According to that, Marlene's children will be Jews."

"Don't think about it." Fogel closed his eyes. "I know the outcome." Jews, the color of ashes. No-longer Jews. Haman! The noise started up again. This time Fogel didn't whirl his noisemaker. He kept his eyes shut. Bright colors reeled across his field of vision, neon colors—purple, glassy green, various reds, as in a film gone out of control.

Marlene is enjoying. Steven is enjoying.

Enjoy!

Purim. A wife, a husband. Enjoy! Has not Dr. Wax said: Worry is bad! Depression is bad! Has not Fogel himself decided: cheerfulness, smiling, laughter! Enjoy! Besides, how much longer?

FOGEL PUT ON his new shoes. He took Lillian's Leatherette jewelry box out of the bedroom dresser, her side, and held it in front of her, open. "Dress!" he commanded. "Adorn!" He reached in and pulled out the gold fleur-de-lys brooch he had given Lillian on her fortieth birthday. Then he found one of the matching earrings which he had bought for her when she turned forty-one.

Lilies for Lillian. This was a birthday tradition that Fogel had established. Sometimes Easter lilies (April 14 was Lillian's birthday); sometimes lilies of the valley. Always lilies, plus one other gift: sometimes a cookbook, one year a book called *Love Poems for Reading Aloud*, one year a Hula-Hoop which they played with at night after the children were asleep.

"Live it up!" In *The Times* he'd read about a fine new Indian restaurant right off Fifth Avenue, Gaylord. "While you're still in the pink."

Lillian smiled suspiciously. "What I'd really enjoy is a drive up to Boston this weekend to see Marlene. Seventh month! I bet she's enormous. The new apartment, I'm dying to see it."

"Never mind Marlene." Fogel rummaged through the jewelry box searching for the other earring. "Enjoy! A movie. So what, a line, waiting. This is the city."

"HAIR!" Fogel said as they got off the train at Grand Central. "Now in film." For a professor was it not prudent to keep abreast of youth culture? *Jugendkraft. Jugendkultur.*

"Aquarius." In the theater, Fogel put his arm around Lillian's shoulder. They were sitting only a few rows from the back, far over on the side because there had been hundreds of people in line waiting in a cold drizzle to get into the 9:10 showing. With gentlemanly courtesy, Fogel had put his hand above Lillian's head to protect her hairdo. "A little wet. So what! Aquarius. Enjoy."

Sitting in a back row was better. Sitting in a front row gave headaches, even to someone without neurosis. Not neurosis, tumor. Certainly tumor. Fogel was finished, he was finishing. Color flowed over the screen; music gushed out of the speakers; the movie was ending; electric colors: reds, greens, blazing yellows.

"Look." Fogel rubbed his hand against the theater-seat upholstery, plush. "Look, like colors from a machine." Color such as he had expected to see in his brain picture. But what did he see? Only one color, gray, camp gray. Should he now spoil Lillian's pleasure by mentioning the brain scan at Mount Sinai? No, no, he should not.

"Beautiful colors." The noisy music stopped. Suddenly, among the emptying theater seats, it was as quiet as death. Fogel's head hurt. "Interesting music." He helped Lillian on with her coat. "Beautiful."

Usually after seeing a musical, Lillian walked out of the theater humming. Tonight she didn't hum. "Steven. If only Steven could do that. Someday, maybe."

Fogel knew what this meant: Lillian was unhappy about Marlene. The movie was interracial.

"Never mind Steven. Now what do you want, dancing? Dancing, coffee, whatever you prefer? Never mind Steven. Tonight we worry only about if we catch the train."

"Hello! Look who's here!" In the clogged, noisy lobby, Terry was touching Fogel, touching Lillian. "I bet you're Lillian."

"How do you you do?" Lillian edged away from her.

"From my group." Fogel's accent became stronger. His Rs went almost out of control. "Terry. From the psychiatrist. Terry." With Terry was a balding young man with a mustache, Jewish, Len, an enthusiastic shaker of hands, also an enjoyer.

"How is your head today?" Terry stroked Fogel's shoulder.

"My head." Fogel wagged it first to the right side and then to the left. "My head."

Just a few days earlier, Terry had hugged him in Dr. Wax's waiting room. "I just learned about a new way to cure your headaches." She had kissed him on the forehead, lightly. "But Pauline says you should have used your fireplace. That really would have worked."

"My fireplace is never used." Fogel had helped Terry off with her coat as he often did when visiting Dr. Wax. Again, a many-needles. "My headaches are never cured."

"Here's the new way: Sing! Sing an octave and then the next one. Keep going up and down the scales. Soon you'll find a note that makes your head feel better. Then hold that note and keep singing it. Your head will clear."

"I am not a singer." This fact had always caused Fogel regret.

"Sing. Come on, sing. Don't be shy." Terry had started at the bottom of the scale and had glided her way up and then down again, a siren. She found one note and held on to it. Then she had stopped and sent it out again. "Aaaaaaaaaah! That's it for me. That's the one. I sing it and my head clears. It's wonderful when you have a cold. Aaaaaaaaaah!"

"Sh." Fogel had covered his lips with his fingertips. "Sh. A doctor's office."

Terry had stuck out her tongue at the door between the waiting room and Dr. Wax's private office. "Aaaaaaaaaah," she sang again. "It's soundproof in there."

"Aaaaaaaaaah!" In front of the theater now, she was playing the siren again. She winked at Fogel. "Why is an elephant big, gray and wrinkled?"

86

"This is a joke?"

Terry began stroking Fogel's back. "I know a fabulous place around the corner on Sixty-first," she said. "Let's go there and have some coffee."

"An elephant?" Lillian seemed to smile. "I wouldn't know."

"Because—" Provocatively, Terry touched her upper teeth with the tip of her tongue. Didn't her boyfriend mind this, all the touching, all the flirting with other men? Was this the sort of girl Steven spent his nights with in California? "Because—you'll like this—because if it were small, white and smooth, it would be an aspirin."

For headaches, they send a man to a psychiatrist. For headaches, they make jokes. Big, gray and wrinkled—this is Fogel's brain. "Certainly coffee," Fogel said to Terry. "Why not coffee?"

Also why not jokes?

In Dr. Wax's group, jokes served a therapeutic function: They taught the neurotics to take their neuroses lightly. When Annabel happily announces: "I lost three pounds," Schwartz says, "Watch out!" and makes a pinching gesture at her heavy behind. "I'll be coming after you." But then he points at shy Macy. "You can start practicing with him." Macy blushes. The entire group can see: Macy is pleased. "Look at him!" Terry calls out when Macy blushes. "He's willing. He wants to, watch out for Macy." Annabel pushes Schwartz's hand away. She smiles at Macy. "But I'm a good girl, I am." Schwartz moves his hand toward her again. "Or maybe Chaim." "No." Fogel ventures to wink at Terry. "I have sworn to be faithful to my wife."

There have been many jokes about headaches. After Charlotte, sugar-voiced, asks, "Does your head hurt today?" and Fogel's often-pained head shakes from side to side to answer no, Charlotte might attempt a joke: "Wrong! You still have a headache, but it's of the painless type." Or Schwartz might say that his neighbor in Cedarhurst, who manufactures plastic bottles for an aspirin company, will give Fogel a thousand dollars for an endorsement. Or, best of all, Terry might stroke his forehead with light, cool fingers and say, "I cured it." "Thank you," Fogel would answer. "But it hurts again. I need another cure." And then he would point to other parts of his body—not exactly point, but make vague gestures that were clear enough; she would understand. Is Schwartz the only sexy in the group?—and say, "It hurts. I have a sudden pain. Maybe you could cure that too." And Terry would laugh. Not a "Ha-ha!" Not a "No way!" A genuine laugh.

"Certainly coffee," Fogel said again. "Why not coffee?"

"Where are we going? Where are they leading us?" Lillian asked in Yiddish as they walked behind Terry and her friend along the wet, glistening Third Avenue sidewalk.

"Sixty-one," Fogel answered, in Yiddish too. "You heard also. Sixty-one."

"Wait!" Terry's boyfriend, Len, held out his hand just as Fogel was raising to his lips the cup of coffee he'd ordered, The East Side Swinger, Rum Flavor. The coffee shop was overheated and overcrowded, filled with "elegants"—this was what people who dressed too fashionably were called in Lvov. "Wait!" Len gave Terry an alert, significant glance. Terry put her hand on her forehead and said, "Oh, my God!" She hunched forward.

"Wait. What do you mean, wait?" The cup shook in Fogel's hand. "Why wait?"

Lillian raised her cup—Coffee au Mint Chocolate—and sipped it. "Magnificent," she murmured. No one stopped her. Fogel put down his cup.

"He shouldn't have coffee." Len shook his head up and down as if he were agreeing with himself. "Caffeine poisoning."

"I read that too." Terry put her hand on Lillian's. "Keep him away from coffee. I feel terrible. I shouldn't have suggested this place. Do you like blackberry tea? Chamomile? One of those?"

"I always drink coffee." Fogel raised his cup again, drank and then exhaled in satisfaction. "I already gave up chocolate because it is associated with headaches. Not coffee." Why not enjoy? Why always worry-worry? "Delicious. I had years without coffee. Now I have coffee."

"Live without it for a week. Two weeks." Terry reached now for Fogel's hand and squeezed it. "Maybe the headaches will go away. Try it."

"Plus this," Len said solemnly. "Biofeedback."

"Bio-what?" Lillian said.

"Bio-phooey!" Fogel snapped his fingers. "Bio-nothing! To me this is nothing new. In the camps, this is how Jews survived." This was how Fogel had been warmed on cold nights—by watching color-fire. This was how Fogel had cleaned the latrine floor on the day when he was forced to be a pisslicker—by ignoring. "Now it is called biofeedback."

"Maybe Alignment." Len straightened up in his chair. "Maybe Centering or Rebirthing."

If not Jupiter, Baal. If not Baal, Marduk.

Len motioned the waitress over to the table. He pointed at Fogel. "One chamomile tea here." Then he turned to Fogel. "Acupuncture."

"Macrobiotics, but—" Terry held out her hand toward Lillian again. This time, however, she didn't touch. "That involves a big life-style change. You know, cooking."

89

Len glared at her. "Macrobiotics is shit. Maybe he needs, like, a Master. Muktananda. Darshan Singh."

"Bliss," Terry said cooperatively. She was happy to entertain any suggestion.

A Master. Fogel's great-grandfather had had a Master, the Belzer Rebbe. Food from the Master's plate was holy. Fogel's mother had told stories. "Eat," she would murmur if Fogel failed to finish his supper. "Pretend it's from the Rebbe's plate." In the camps, when she was smoke and he was skin, Fogel remembered these words.

"Biofeedback is shit." Fogel defiantly took another sip of coffee. "A Master is shit. Cooking style also is shit. This includes kosher." Shit is a word he had never, even once, spoken in front of Lillian. As if she wouldn't understand it, he turned to her and said, "Dreck."

BUT LILLIAN went to the library and found a book, *You Are a Guru*. She forced Fogel to read it.

On a Saturday morning, he began.

Step one: Touch your head. Touch each of your fingers and toes. Touch your private parts.

Step two: Touch the floor of your living room, the walls, the houseplants. Go outdoors. Look at the sky. Look at the earth. Look at the trees on the earth. Touch. Look. Look. Touch. You are one with nature.

Fogel went into the living room, to the bay window, and began to stroke Lillian's houseplants, first the shining green leaves of the big philodendron; then the dark leaves of the gloxinia, a velvety, sensuous plant. Outdoors, in the green plaid jacket he wore when he raked leaves, he inspected the wintry sky over White Plains. There, invisible in the grayness, the Angel of Death was flying. Again today, a no-coffee breakfast. Again today also, a gouger.

90

Though the jacket was made of wool, Fogel began to shiver. He forced himself to stop: It was not suitable for a guru to worry about the Angel of Death.

Quickly, he looked down at the spongy earth and then hurried across the yard toward a tree, a leafless maple, standing half on his property, half on his neighbor's. Not only men suffer, trees suffer too. Trees feel pain. Trees get sick and die. Blights fly through the air, cancers. First the leaves go, then the branches, then finally the roots; and then after they are dead, come termites.

The maple tree in the yard was strong and healthy-looking, however. Nobody was watching. Fogel leaned his head against the rough trunk, his arm went around the trunk; he wouldn't kiss it, maybe another time. Who kisses trees? And why should anyone do such a thing? With the palm of his hand brushing lightly against the tree trunk, Fogel felt the ridges, the tree print. No two trees are alike. God has made each one of them different. Not God, nature. Nobody was watching. Fogel wasn't being observed, but if he was, so what! Fogel kissed the tree trunk. As soon as his lips touched bark, his headache disappeared. It was gone, and his cheek was next to the bark. His hand caressed the bark, his arms grasped the trunk. "Father," Fogel whispered in Yiddish. "Father, help me!" Then he whispered the same words in German.

His own father was now among the trees. Maybe he was a tree. He had been smoke, he had become air and then rain, falling into the earth, all his carbon, all his hydrogen. He was a tree in Europe. Pressing his head against the tree trunk, Fogel made a small animal-like cry, a caw. Headache was chopping at him.

Upstairs in his bedroom, Fogel stretched out on the carpeting, ashamed. It was comfortable—high-pile broadloom,

91

the best. Prostrating himself, he brushed his lips against the carpet and kissed it. He opened his mouth. With his tongue, he tasted the carpet. Thready. Dry. Like a dog, he ran his tongue over the carpet wool. Now he was a ruglicker. *"Je crois,"* he whispered, *"je crois,"* using the words of Voltaire, the great skeptic who, finally succumbing to supernatural power, climbed the mountain and saw the view and took off his hat and bowed down to the ground and called out, "I believe in you, powerful God." Fogel's tears wet the carpet. *"Je crois,"* he whispered again, and then he said, *"Credo,"* and then, *"Ani Ma-amin."* The carpeting wasn't only high-pile. It was sky-blue. It soaked up his tears and soaked up the tiny hurt sounds he was making. Was this the behavior of a guru? Believe in your own powers, in your own natural power. At biofeedback, Fogel was a failure.

"God! God! What happened?" Fogel was lying on the floor, collapsed. Lillian walked by, she saw him, she ran in, she crouched over him. "Chaim?" This wasn't a question. It was wailing, woe, the gnashing of teeth.

The beloved rolled over; he looked up at her, his eyes cloudy, his mouth open. He was unshaven. "You are interrupting me."

"God!" Lillian was still gasping. She was wearing her red slacks, the ones Fogel especially liked, the ones that showed smoothness over her thighs. "God! What's the matter?"

"Biofeedback. I am trying to cure my headache."

"On the floor? Lying down like a dead man?" Lillian pressed her cheek against his. "I shouldn't say this. No! But you terrified me." She put her hand on his shoulder. She kissed him, on the lips. He rested his hand on her thigh. Slowly, lightly, hopefully, he began to stroke.

As it is written: Rejoice in the wife of your youth. As it is commanded: Honor the Sabbath.

All of nature sings praises to Me on the Sabbath. Even the trees and the holy arks made from trees sing praises, and the holy scroll posts and the spice-holders, the garlands, the crowns, the carved cherubim and tablets, the gilded wooden lions that guard the holy arks. Pale and breathless, Fogel tries to sing praises too. But his tree is fallen. Dry and dying, what is he now? Merely paper in a book, less than paper, less than the trees out of which he's been made.

Can Fogel, a pagan, sing praises? A witch-visitor, an idol-worshiper? Like his idol Voltaire, he says, "I believe," but that's only because his head hurts. I, even I, do not believe him. Trees can be transformed into garlands, into arks and scroll posts, into spice-holders and cherubim. Can Fogel be transformed? Or is it too late? What could be made of him now? Maybe a lampshade? But it's too late, even for that.

IX

Headaches, Nazis, a psychiatrist, a son, a daughter, yet Chaim Fogel survives. The tree is not yet fallen, the pillar still rises.

"Lillian," Fogel breathed as he straddled her, satisfyingly at last, in bed that night, his elbows aching from the strain of supporting himself. "Lillian, do you love me?"

For answer Lillian groaned, she clasped him tight, her thighs pressed against his legs. Fogel could feel her flesh flowing around him. "Do I!" she gasped. "Do I!" But the answer wasn't yes.

"Lillian, do you love me?" Fogel asked again at breakfast time a few days later, the two of them sitting opposite each other in the sunny kitchen nibbling on homemade streusel loaf and sipping blackberry tea. It was a Tuesday. They had only six minutes left before driving to the station.

"What kind of a question is that? Am I doing something wrong? Is it about Marlene? Or is this part of biofeedback?"

"I'm curious." Did not Schwartz's wife frequently express her hot desire for Schwartz? Did not even Annabel's husband daily give Annabel reassurance of his love? "I wish to know. A simple question."

"At breakfast time?"

Instead of answering, Fogel got up from the kitchen table to retire into the downstairs bathroom.

"Listen, if there's something wrong, if there's something you don't feel like talking to me about," Lillian said as the car was idling in front of the White Plains station, "tell me about it." She turned off the motor. "You're so troubled." She reached over and touched his cheek with her fingertips. "You're still so upset about Marlene. Talk to me. If something else is worrying you—the headaches, the psychiatrist— tell me. I'm a very understanding person."

"Ha!" Fogel leaned over to kiss her on the lips, extra firm. He got out of the car. His heart was breaking. His daughter had married a Gentile. What kind of a woman was he himself married to, the mother of such a daughter, a woman who refused to tell her husband that she loved him, even while they were making love, even though he might be dying from headaches? What kind of a woman was this? A slut?

And once so loving. Once so kindhearted. So sympathetic when Fogel was first out of the displaced camp and finally in-placed in America, living on 112th Street in a room off a long dusty apartment hallway lined with students' rooms. "Are you pious too?" Lillian had inquired cautiously after she and Fogel were introduced by her friend Bernice who also lived in the apartment. Fogel was making tea in the apartment's common kitchen—gloomy, neon-lit, roachy, and kosher because some of the roomers were pious Jews.

"Never." A one-word answer.

Why only one word? Was Fogel rude? Was Fogel shy? Was he blind: hips, cheeks, hair, arms?

No. It was because at that time Fogel was a man of little conversation. His answers to questions were brief. This was the reason: His accent caused him shame. This was a second reason: Before his eyes, people had died. Therefore, in his throat, the words these people had spoken died too—German, Polish, Yiddish, all dead. English words refused to rise to take their place. Why should this be? English was a language of high reputation. Yet what flavor did it really have with its inflexible verbs, its genderless and uncoupling nouns?

"Never say never." Lillian winked at Fogel. In time this wink—was it really a wink, or was it perhaps only a wink in his imagination?—would make words spurt out of him again.

How he had loved her! How thankful he was he had met her! How glad he was that she had dared to knock on his door when she came again to visit her friend Bernice. "I hope I'm not intruding." "Intruding" was a word unfamiliar to Fogel. Nevertheless, he bowed and welcomed her into his room with a sweeping seigneurial gesture—he was taking a course entitled "The Age of Louis XIV"—and she smiled at him—a girl with long dark hair, full-breasted.

"Bernice said you might discuss something with me. A poem I wrote. About—" Jewish hair. Jewish eyes. Lillian held her breath. "About concentration camps."

"I do not speak about camps."

"Then I won't show you the poem." And Lillian stepped backward, toward the doorway.

A poem helped language learning. Breast: feminine. Camp: neuter. Death: masculine. Fogel took the paper and read.

> Ashes, ashes, ashes, ashes, ashes—
> Whither and Why?
> Jews come to Auschwitz
> Only to die.
> Youths at Treblinka, maidens at Maidanek

"At Maidanek, maidens. This is my sister."
Lillian stared downward at the poem Fogel was holding.

How shyly she had stood in the doorway! How tenderly her eyes had closed when he told her of his sister! How much he had wanted to embrace her! Let Schwartz be unfaithful to his wife! Let Charlotte marriage-break! Let Terry play! Neurotics. Not so Fogel.

"Also my mother, my father: 1943." Fogel handed the paper back to Lillian. "A beautiful poem, but not correct. Not every Jew in Auschwitz only to die, I did not die."

"Bergen-Belsen, I was told." Lillian folded the paper, carefully, as if her greatest concern were creases.

"Correct. For me Auschwitz was a transit camp. Now I know this. Whither?" Fogel almost smiled. He had spoken of Maidanek, he had said the word Belsen, and he almost smiled. "Whither? This means what for?"

"Correct," Lillian said.

"A poet!" Fogel grasped Lillian's hand and held on to it. "Heine, sonnet to his mother? 'Gentle heart which loves me with blindness'?" Lillian nodded her head slowly from side to side. This meant she was sad. This meant she had never heard the sonnet. "My mother made me learn it. She gave me money if I would say it to her."

"Recite it to me."

"Tomorrow," Fogel said. Lillian moved her head again, this time up and down, not from side to side; this time quickly not slowly.

"Do you know English poems?" Lightly, Lillian put her own hand over Fogel's. " 'Come live with me, and be my love.' Marlowe." She took a deep breath. " 'Hark how the minstrels 'gin to shrill aloud.' " Her hands were small; her fingernails were adorned with a rosy, female-color polish. " 'Their merry music that resounds from far,' Spenser's wedding poem."

And now—could it be possible?—a slut.

" 'Gin to shrill aloud." Reading these words improved knowledge of English. Familiarity with these words benefited a man. Once a week, in Fogel's private room, reading the heavy books Lillian carried with her, two volumes, *The College Survey of English Literature,* many love poems, Fogel held Lillian's hand; he stroked her back. He caressed her shoulders. From time to time even he was allowed to fondle her breasts.

Once a week, poetry. Once a week, Lillian.

And once a day, a choice: riding uptown to CCNY to study crusaders, emperors, tendencies, movements, bibliographies, Voltaire, Rousseau, Gotthold Ephraim Lessing, the admirer of the Jews; or walking uptown instead, twenty-five blocks. A five-cent piece for subway fare, a five-cent piece for candy. After nights enclosed at his employment-place, the necktie shop in Times Square, among the repps and paisleys, among the tourists, drunks, smart guys and perverts, Fogel's choice was to walk, to enjoy sweetness: Mounds Bar, creamy coconut flavor; Clark Bar, crunchy peanut-butter taste, enfolded— this was the word the advertising-speakers used—enfolded in smooth milk chocolate. Formerly, who could imagine such foods? "I have one each day. I eat," he told Lillian. "Do you know why?"

"You were so emaciated." There were tears in Lillian's eyes. "Now you want to be fat."

"Incorrect. Here is the correct answer. Eating so makes me certain of this: It is not wrong to be a survivor." The next week Lillian brought him a gift, a box tied with a pink ribbon and filled with twenty-four candies, different kinds: Hershey, Nestlé, Bit O' Honey, M & M, Oh Henry, all American except for one Jewish, halvah.

How Fogel's sister would have loved them! "What was

her name?" Lillian asked. "I feel I know her." Her name was Mira.

"Did she have light hair too like you?" Fogel's hair was not the color of an Aryan's hair, fair. But it was not black like Lillian's hair.

"No." Fogel ran his fingers through Lillian's hair. "Like this. Dark."

With poetry and sweetness—this was how Lillian had won his heart.

"I DREAMED about you last night," Terry whispered the Tuesday evening after their coffee-shop rendezvous. She spoke these words to Fogel in a saucy, intimate voice—to Fogel, not to Schwartz, not to Len. Fogel raised his chin and, looking directly into Terry's eyes, audaciously inquired: "What was the dream? How did I appear? Exactly what were we doing?" even though Terry had not admitted that she herself was in the dream. Perhaps these questions were too direct. Perhaps they were too forceful or went beyond the bounds of discretion. Terry didn't answer. All she did was smile. Then, still smiling, she bit her lower lip. And then, then, when Fogel ventured to ask yet another question— "Was it a pleasurable dream?"—she blushed. There was his answer. The dream was about sex.

In Dr. Wax's office, there was no poetry, but on the other hand there was always sex. Sex was in the air, just as it had been in the camp yard during the months after liberation. Was it not Helvétius who remarked that men who have escaped doom preoccupy themselves with romance? Perhaps the members of Dr. Wax's psychoneurotic group had escaped doom, for they spoke about sex frequently, without modesty and without shame. Macy, the silent youth, was encouraged to masturbate daily. Annabel was promised that if she lost thirty pounds and belly-danced enticingly in front of her husband, she could rid herself of jealousy. Fogel himself had been told that headaches and children-worries do not necessarily make a man's marital sex-life deteriorate. All he had to do was swing a little with Lillian or, if he preferred, with someone else.

For not only was sex in the air, marital infidelity was in the air as well. Already, Terry had enjoyed two affairs with married men, one of them a high-school classmate of her father's. "That was my most wonderful lifetime experience," she had confessed to Fogel one Tuesday in Dr. Wax's waiting room, not even looking away as she talked.

Schwartz was a roué as well as a transvestite. Furthermore, he was a bragger. "I give it to my secretary once a week and to my wife twice. And to anyone else who wants it too. But does any of it make me happy?" His freckles darkened. "I could make a dozen a week and be all dolled up like a movie star, but I'd still be torn up inside." Infidelity had brought Schwartz grief, not joy.

Charlotte also. Formerly, Charlotte had carried on a secret love affair with her next-door neighbor on West Eighty-sixth Street. Then her husband had discovered it and divorced her. "Maybe you go into panics on the subway because you're afraid of your diffuse sexual impulses," Schwartz had once said to Charlotte during a group session, wagging his thick finger at her as if she were a naughty girl. Sexual impulses! Was Schwartz flirting? No, Schwartz was not flirting. Schwartz was attempting to make a serious psychological analysis. And he was correct. Charlotte admitted having diffuse sexual impulses. "But I never think that anyone's attractive on the subway."

Occasionally Fogel himself had diffuse sexual impulses. No, not occasionally sexual impulses. Now—the truth must be admitted—frequently sexual impulses. But infidelity, never! Adultery, never! He had made his vow. He had declared his love: He would be faithful to Lillian always. No matter where he might be—in Rio at carnival time, on a desert island with Marilyn Monroe, in Greenwich Village alone with Terry, even with Terry, certainly even with Terry—he would not slip, he would not fail; he would soil himself, his underwear, his own hands first. He would be faithful. It was inhuman.

But what good is fidelity to a man like Fogel, a man being killed by headache, a man whose own wife—the receptacle of his sexual impulses, the object of his heartfelt purity-vow—suddenly decides to become a slut?

Fogel's wife, the wife of his youth, his helper, Madame-behind-his-back. At dinner she tried to act normally, pretending that nothing unusual had happened. When she wanted to know what time it was, instead of looking at the clock hanging on the kitchen wall, she stretched across the table to squint at the new digital watch she had recently given him.

"Why a present?" Fogel had inquired when he saw it sitting, gift-wrapped, beside his dinner plate one evening. "It's not even my birthday." Was this not a logical question? "I don't know. I just felt like buying you a present." Was this a believable answer? Or was it perhaps an indication of a guilty slut-conscience? And when she finished the dinner dishes, she sauntered into the den while Fogel was sitting glancing through a magazine. She looked pleased with herself, satisfied.

She interrupted his reading. "Your psychoanalysis is making you preoccupied. A man came in today to put on the

101

new storm door and you didn't even notice it. You walked into the kitchen, right through it, and didn't even say a thing."

There was a triumph-look on Lillian's face. What should he say? What should he do? Sneak home at noon like a cinema-husband and surprise her sweating on the living-room couch with the delivery man? In flagrante delicto. A woman who bears false witness. The strange woman, her kisses are sweet, her lips drip honey, her eyes are like pits. She traffics in secret even within her husband's walls, and as for him, what he doesn't know won't hurt him.

"I understand what's bothering you," Lillian said. "But you're not being fair to Marlene. How would you like it if your family refused to accept me." Suddenly she caught sight of the magazine Fogel was reading. "What have you got that for? Trash! Why are you reading that?" The magazine was *Playboy*. Once Steven had purchased a subscription, only once, but the magazine kept coming year after year. If Lillian got to it first, she threw it out.

"Come, sit on my lap," Fogel whispered. Shouldn't a man dying of brain tumor hug and fondle a woman? Shouldn't he kiss her, on the mouth, on the cheek, both firmly and gently, before the tumor destroys him—and then there are no more fondles, no more kisses? Shouldn't he touch, wasn't this his need, even more than it was Steven's need, Steven's or Terry's, the young? Shouldn't such a man continue life-enhancing activities and attempt to enjoy the few days left to him? Is it not incumbent upon him to ignore unworthy suspicions about his wife? Unworthy suspicions, maybe ridiculous suspicions. "You could read it with me." Fogel patted his lap. "Who knows what it would lead to." Once a man turns fifty-two, fifty-four, he slows down. But for her what did it matter, one more time? Could she get tired? Before dinner, after dinner, before menopause, after menopause. In Lvov there had been a notorious woman: Leah All-day they called her. Why not in White Plains too?

"Let me call Boston now to arrange a visit. We have to show Teddy we accept him." Lillian sat down, not on Fogel's lap, but not at the opposite end of the sofa either. She put her hand on his arm. "Chaim, in two months you'll be a grandfather."

"We ourselves should have another baby. A new little Jew, maybe a boy, maybe a girl." Moving his left hand very slowly, Fogel covered up a picture in the magazine.

Is this the act of a man immersed in the Enlightenment? No, it is the act of a man who spends his time with psychoneurotics. Thus he becomes paranoid about his wife. Thus, at an advanced age, he makes bizarre baby-fathering statements.

"Too late." Lillian's hand slid away from Fogel's arm. "For me to have a baby now would be a miracle. Marlene will have the babies."

"Be fruitful and multiply. Every baby is a miracle. Jewish."

"For me a double miracle." Lillian leaned forward and pinched Fogel's cheek. Today her fingernails were polished. "You know why."

"I already know miracles." Boldly, Fogel moved his hand and peered down at the magazine. "Forget Marlene. No Jewish babies from Marlene."

Lillian sighed, making her breasts rise and then subside. She snapped her fingers at the magazine. *"Playboy!* These are the girls who can still have babies." Her voice cracked. "Me, it's too late, almost a grandmother. I already had babies." Suddenly her eyes glittered with fury. "Who is it? Who? A student?" She rubbed her hands back and forth

103

over her thighs. "Tell me. Who? In your psychiatry group, that crazy girl? A student? Who? How many times?"

"Imagination." Fogel groaned. "Imagination." In California a blond, a bunny, a starlet, stirs in bed twining her legs around Steven's legs, whispering, "I love you, I love you."

"I'm sorry. My apologies. That's something I shouldn't have said." Lillian's right hand, resting on her lap, became a fist. With her left hand, she began tapping at it. "I shouldn't even think it, but there's been so much tension in this house. Such a long winter! We should have taken a vacation. You want to go away next winter, we'll go away. Christmas vacation, maybe between terms, January. Florida, I'll make a reservation, this time in a motel."

"Make it, go ahead, make it. What do I care?" Fogel looked away, down toward the magazine still resting on the couch.

"You'd rather go to India?"

There was the March bunny, wearing only a loincloth and a diamond in her nose, her arms raised to heaven like a sun-worshiping yogi. A triumph of color printing. Her skin, her lips, looked more alive than Lillian's. And Lillian was sitting right there, Lillian who could actually be touched, Lillian who was no bunny anymore. Had she ever been a bunny? Her lips had lines, little crevices, chasms, cuts, clefts, canyons, bump, bump, up and down. Fogel loved them, he hated them. Someday he might run his tongue along them to find out which. Could he kiss bunnies?

"I don't want anymore. I want easy. Someplace quiet. Someplace warm."

Suddenly Fogel's arms felt chilled, his chest, his legs, the usually warm place between his legs. Icy America was drying him up. He should never have come to America. He should have gone to the land of Israel, to the heat. In the displaced persons camp he'd had the chance. A different temperature, a different Lillian Fogel, different children, authentic Jews, Jews who marry Jews. Now he had ice drops for tears, his hair was icicles, ice hanging under his arms and between his legs: frozen lumps, ice stones; his fingernails, glistening rinks; his mouth, an ice cave, his eyes—better not think of them, they were transparent. Fogel sat staring at Lillian. For this woman, only recently, he had had sex feelings. Now they were gone. Was it possible for a man suddenly to forget his sex feelings? Could such a thing be? Was it a result of brain tumor? Nervously, Fogel tried to remember sex feelings. Alas, he could not. Now, finally, were they gone? "I could move to Miami," he said. "Dade Community College. A two-year school."

"I couldn't go. Forget it." Lillian's voice chilled with urgency. "You couldn't drag me out of White Plains with a bulldozer." Stiffly, she braced her back against the sofa.

Was it a construction worker, then? A perspirer, a digger, his fingernails never clean? He places his hands on her. Couldn't she even wait until her husband died? Widow Fogel. Then, quick, eight months, a year after the funeral, off for weekends to a resort hotel. An evening of dancing with a retired schoolteacher, maybe a union organizer, maybe a minor functionary from a Jewish organization. They would strain at it, she would giggle, she would be nostalgic, remembering her husband, the late Fogel. The next morning she would cry. And she would go again.

Was she even waiting until he was dead.

A coincidence: The Playboy Colloquium, March, was entitled "Death and Sex." "You could die," it had said. "You could die before you finish reading this page." Page fifty-three.

As soon as he had seen that, Fogel had stopped reading

and put the magazine down on his lap. "Feh!" he said. "Feh!" It didn't scare him, death didn't scare him, a European; idle threats. He had survived Nazis. What could happen now? But then, suddenly self-conscious, he had grabbed on to the magazine again and continued reading, fast, his eyes skimming the rest of the page, three columns of type, small print, boring, about God knows what—death, sex, American Society, the Individual—Where Is He Going? Not even when he reached the bottom of the page did Fogel lift his eyes, not even when it came time to turn the page, because there was more to the article. He turned over the page, to what?

Fifty-four, his age.

"You could stay in White Plains," he said to Lillian. "And me, I like warm, I could transfer to Miami."

"Discuss this with your psychiatrist, not with me." Lillian's lips became narrow, white. "Ridiculous! Of course not. No."

Ridiculous!

But did she mean it?

She meant it. Or maybe she didn't mean it. Paranoia was a disease of old age. Already Fogel felt the first symptoms. And no wonder. Who could he trust when the hour came? Who would stand with him?

Till death do us part.

You don't have to wait that long for a wall to come between man and wife. One false move and that's it. It rises up, quicker than you can say "community property." Even God can't knock it down.

Suddenly, surprisingly, Lillian stood up. "Ay, ay!" she sang, "Ay, ay! Have you ever been to the tropics?" She snapped her fingers. "Ay, ay! You're becoming crazy, Chaim. Ay, Ay!" She shrugged, first one shoulder, then the other, each motion carrying along with it a breast which bobbed before Fogel's eyes. At the court of Louis XVI, Benjamin Franklin had noted it: Women age downward. When the face has wrinkles, the body is still desirable. She swiveled her hips, she danced, first back away from him and then forward, toward him— Is this appropriate, a fifty-year-old woman? "Ay, ay! Ay, ay! It's the South American way.

"Ay, ay, Chaim. What do you want? You don't know what you want. Midlife crisis—you're turning crazy. Maybe from the psychiatrist." Awkwardly, she moved her hips back and forth, side to side. To his shock, Fogel discovered that he was getting excited. So! His sex feelings had not perished after all.

Ay! Ay! Is this what it means, erratic behavior? One day hating Lillian, one day loving Lillian. One day enlightened, the next next day a witch-customer, a ruglicker. Is this a case of delayed midlife crisis? Maybe it's a case of early senile dementia. Why is it happening? The questions gathered, they lumped, suddenly they spurted out of Fogel's eyes: tears.

He put his head down and hid his face with his arms. He was foolish, he was sorry. "What's the matter with me? What's wrong with me?" Lillian was holding his head, her breast soft, his skull hard. This was not a bunny. This was a woman he could touch, a woman he could kiss. With such a wife, no man was finished. She was the one who rescued him from the ashes, out of the work camp, the death camp, the concentration, the relocation. She was the one who convinced him that, though once a pisslicker, he could still kiss. Four years in the camps and no tears shed. Now, suddenly, tears. What's going on?

Why such behavior?

The God of Abraham, Isaac and Jacob knows the answer.

X

I think you should really try Spiritual Transformation—Master Darshan, Master Buddha." Fogel was sitting on a soft, round chair in Len's shabby loft, visiting Terry while Len was at his yoga session. "Or try Lord Krishna." Fogel closed his eyes. "I think Master Satsrananda is helping me." When Fogel opened one eye, Terry was smiling beatifically. "I went to see him with Len last weekend up in the Catskills." She leaned forward and brushed her fingertips over Fogel's forehead. "It was beautiful. He touched me just like that."

"Do it again." Fogel opened both eyes.

Again Terry's touch skimmed over Fogel's forehead. "Dr. Wax never touches. Touching is important. Usually Satsrananda touches people with a peacock feather, but he touched me with his own hand." Terry's mouth puckered with satisfaction. "Here!" Terry reached for a piece of paper and set it on Fogel's lap, right on top of what Dr. Wax often referred to as his "member." "You ought to read this."

On the paper there were two pictures, one of Satsrananda, a wispy, dark-skinned man, and the other of his cult emblem, a circle enclosing two hands raised in prayer. Around the edge of the circle were the words: Thou Art That Thou Art.

Tolerantly, Fogel inspected the paper. Then, politely, he handed it back to Terry. And then, as befits a professor of history, he interpreted its meaning. "A revival of paganism is going on. God is dead. Here we have a characteristic manifestation of the pagan revival." Perhaps this analysis was something Terry would understand. She seemed to because she began to smile again.

"Phenomena of this type mark the end of the monotheistic experiment and are a consequence of the Enlightenment, related to Lessing's pantheism"—Fogel spoke slowly—"although superficially and with certain distortions."

Now Terry was listening attentively. Finally, Fogel had captured her attention. Finally, he could advance her intellectual development. Terry was watching him, Terry was smiling at him.

"This paper says 'Thou Art That Thou Art.' What did the monotheistic God declare to Moses?"

Terry let the paper drop to the floor. She shrugged. Her mouth twitched from side to side. Alas, she didn't know the answer.

Fogel supplied the answer. "I will tell you. 'I Am That I Am'—this is what God told Moses."

"You need to be tickled." Suddenly Terry was sitting on Fogel's lap. "That's what I think."

Terry's arms were naked. Gingerly, Fogel put his own arm around her. "Touching is also an aspect of the pagan revival. But an aspect I prefer." Then, boldly, he grasped one of her hands, a tickler.

Terry giggled. "I'm not spiritual all the time. Len is spiritual all the time now."

Under Fogel, the chair was yielding. On top of Fogel, Terry's plumpness was yielding too. Terry kissed Fogel's earlobe. Now it was being kissed. Soon it might be acupunctured. Such is man's fate. Never mind acupuncture! Kisses are not needles. The pagan revival—certainly, a commendable tendency, ditto

109

psychotherapy: they inspire Terry to lap-sit, they inspire Terry to ear-kiss. Terry is his fate. Terry, young as a bunny. In his ear, Terry's breath is warm. In his ear, Terry is whispering, private words, words of comfort. "I can fix you up now. Honest. Pauline told me another way to do it."

Pauline the witch! Better a witch than an acupuncturist with needles.

"What I'm going to do might surprise you, but Pauline said you wouldn't mind."

Terry's tongue slipped in and out of Fogel's ear so quickly it was as if Terry's tongue-wetness, Terry's ear-licking were being felt in Fogel's imagination and not in his ear. But then Terry moved her head away and hid her face against Fogel's shoulder. "Maybe I really shouldn't do this. I mean, it seems funny. You know, I mean, you're not my Romeo or anything."

Romeo! True, never had Fogel been called this name. Therefore instead of speaking—Should he utter romantic Shakespeare language? Could he even do so?—he began lightly stroking Terry's back.

Terry raised her head. "It's not like I'm promiscuous or anything, right?"

"Right."

"But Pauline told me it's OK so long as I do everything she said to do. It'll work if I say every single word exactly right. Like, I wouldn't normally do this, right, but Pauline ..." On Fogel's lap, Terry began to wriggle. Her body weight was comforting. Such weight! Enjoy!

"Len would kill me if he found out. And in his own loft too." This time Terry's eyes twitched from side to side too, along with her mouth. "But then it's OK because the only reason I'm doing something like this is because of your headaches, right?"

There was a silence.

110

"Right?" Terry said again.

"Right," Fogel whispered. His fingers brushed over Terry's back.

"I mean, I feel an obligation to help. I mean because of the group. I think of it as therapy."

Therapy! Fogel is sitting in SoHo with his fly bulging receiving therapy for his headaches while Lillian is walking around the house in White Plains dusting. One part of Fogel can enjoy. It already is enjoying. Terry whispers some words into the palm of her hand. Then she rubs her hand on Fogel's arm. "Where does it hurt?"

Fogel points to one place and then another place and then, daringly, to another place, while Terry sits on his lap, touching, like a spirit. With the tips of her middle fingers, she touches Fogel's forehead and then her own forehead, Fogel's lips and then her own lips, Fogel's shoulder and then her own shoulder. She is touching, she is whispering words into her hand. Softly she blows, at every place he has pointed to, licking like a wind. Those years, his most vigorous years, when a man is at his peak, he was imprisoned, almost dead. Now he is alive, and with a playgirl. She blows softly: Ah, this is enlightenment!

Terry's mouth is open, her plump hand is stroking, her soft fingers with the Indian rings on them, Hindu rings. Voltaire would enjoy. The Poles would enjoy. The Ukrainchik prison guards would enjoy. The Belzer Rebbe would enjoy. The Enlightened Ones of Brody would enjoy. Also King Solomon would enjoy. Honey and milk are under her tongue. Fogel is like a palm tree, like a tower of ivory. King Chimney. King Smokestack. This is therapy. Also it is free. Never mind Blue Cross. Enjoy!

"Finished," Fogel groaned. "Finished."

Terry raised her head. Her eyes were closed, her lips moving like those of a Jew at prayer. Slowly, she opened her eyes. She glanced up at Fogel inquiringly. But why even bother to inquire? Forget it! One result: Yes. One result: No. Easy come, easy go, but it's no easy go for the headache.

Terry blushed. She looked down at the floor and then moved her head so that she was facing away from Fogel, staring at the wall where Len had hung a poster, a picture of the ocean with the word LOVE printed on it. "I wouldn't ever have done that normally. But Pauline said it was the right thing to do." Terry stood up and leaned against the wall. "I certainly did say the words right. Maybe you should see an acupuncturist even though some of them aren't trained right."

"Forget acupuncture! Never mind acupuncture! Your therapeutic treatment is better than acupuncture."

Terry wiped her mouth with the back of her hand, once, and then again, and then once again.

Fogel stood up too. To zip? Not to zip? "Are you embarrassed? Are you regretful?" Modestly, he covered his member with his hand. "I am not embarrassed. On the contrary, I am filled with appreciation and gratitude for your helpfulness." Terry was keeping her face averted. "It is my great desire to give pleasure to you also." Fogel zipped up his pants. "Also gratification, performing an equal courtesy for you."

"No way!" Terry's eyes began twitching from side to side again. Without doubt, an anxiety-mannerism. Anxiety, perhaps regret, perhaps Terry was still unsatisfied. "No way! This was a one-shot. The only reason I did it was because Pauline told me to."

"For everyone gratification is important." A faint, damp, sweaty odor came across the room toward Fogel: Terry in heat. The thought made him hold his breath. Terry's eyes were still looking, not at Fogel, but at the wall behind Fogel.

Did that mean Fogel had to avoid looking at Terry? Certainly not. He should look, he should stare, he should enjoy. A pretty girl, a healthy girl. A girl of many enthusiasms. A girl of Jewish warmth.

"I would like to have a baby with you!" Suddenly these words spilled out of Fogel. "A Jewish child, you are a Jewish girl, also with a Jewish father. Lillian I will give a divorce to." Fogel was standing beside Terry, he was holding on to her wrist, he was stroking her hair. He had not even kissed her. Do you kiss the Empress Catherine the Great? No! She kisses you. But you reach for her breasts, you put your hands on her shoulders, you move your hands downward, both of them, toward the breasts, the beautiful breasts, you refresh your head between them. This brings life.

"Uh-uh!" Quickly, Terry moved away. "Uh-uh! That's a no-no!"

"Why a no-no?"

Folding her arms tight, Terry hugged herself. Her mouth pinched shut. Her eyes closed. "You might feel a lump."

Light was coming into the loft through enormous windows. Fogel turned and looked out. Next door was a factory, also with big windows. In one was a black man, a worker, staring at Fogel and grinning. What he had seen!

"No, no. No babies. No!" Again Terry was giggling, giggling always—an immature girl. Not an intelligent girl, a girl who had once said to Fogel, "I'm into astrology now. Did you know that God is a Scorpio?" and when Fogel lightly responded, "And what is Jesus, a Capricorn?" she replied, "Of course. He was born on December twenty-fifth." A girl who doesn't know when a professor is making jokes. And this is the sort of girl Fogel has invited to be the mother of his child? A joke indeed.

113

"I mean, I like you, but no." Terry's face turned solemn. "Nobody ever asked me that before. Do you really mean it?"

Fogel picked at a fingernail. "Yes."

"With you for a father, the baby would be smart in school."

Fogel was smart in school. Steven and Marlene also were smart. But to what good?

"No. No." Terry shook her head and her shoulders so energetically that her breasts bounced. If there were lumps in her breasts, the lumps bounced too.

OMNIUM ANIMALUM *tristum est.* The philosophers are correct. Therefore, going home, Fogel didn't get off the subway at Grand Central to catch the train for White Plains. Instead he went by his stop, up to Fifty-ninth Street. Then he walked westward to Central Park.

At the park entrance there was a pigeon feather lying on the path in front of him, fallen from the sky like a leaf. Pigeons were not peacocks. Furthermore they brought disease. Nevertheless, Fogel stooped down to pick up the feather. He put it into his pocket. Then he put his hand inside his pocket to rub it between his fingers, to feel its feather-nature. On his left he could see a lake at the bottom of the hill, a lake with the reflection of the Plaza Hotel floating on it, the lake he had longed to visit the night he had almost been mugged by the black man. Once again he longed to visit it.

Why? Because water is life. Because viewing water brings solace to those who are sad. Was it not Rousseau who had said this?

In the camps, whenever rain came down from the heaven,

Fogel was in the habit of sticking out his tongue to catch raindrops, even though the drops contained ashy smoke from the camp chimneys, even though by doing so he, no less than the Schutzstaffel, was devouring the life of Jews. First the Jews had been burned. Then their ashes rose up to the clouds. Then their ashes were swallowed by Chaim Fogel.

"Recite these words," Fogel's grandfather had once commanded him during a summer visit, as they took a Sabbath walk beside the marshy green river on the outskirts of Stoianov. " 'Blessed art Thou, Lord, our God, King of the Universe, Who has created what was created at the time of creation.' This is the beauty-in-nature blessing." Obediently, Fogel had repeated his grandfather's words.

His grandfather let go of Fogel's hand, picked up a pebble and tossed it into the river. "Say these words when you visit the ocean. I myself have never seen the ocean." Certainly by now his grandfather-ashes must have sunk into the ocean. "Not only when you see the ocean," he had added. "When you see a beautiful river or lake, or even a rainbow in a puddle." But when Fogel finally did see the ocean, for eleven days aboard a large steamship, spending many hours inspecting ocean water—sometimes it was chalky blue, sometimes shining green—he was too enlightened to obey his grandfather's command. Now, however, he was no longer an enlightened man. Headache had transformed him. Now he had become one of the superstitious, like Terry and Len, like Pauline, like Satsrananda.

For a moment Fogel stopped walking along the park path and stood still to inspect the lake below him. It was beautiful. Now it was time: He would obey his grandfather's command. He would visit the lake and say the blessing words. So what if superstitious! For the sake of the Jew-ashes he had once devoured, for the sake of the sons and grandsons of the devoured

115

ashes, Chaim Fogel would say these words. Thus would the ash-Jews survive. Thus would they live and not die. Thus Jews will not die. Thus the Jewish People will not die.

Jews, survive! Jews, do not die! Head, do not die! Head, do not kill! Head-pain, give rest! Fogel-head, live!

"Blessed art Thou, Lord, our God!" Fogel walked down the path toward the lake. His throat closed at the word "Lord." "God" was a word he could scarcely say. As he murmured it, he swallowed it. When he recited "Who has created what was created at the time of creation," he pressed the palm of his hand against his forehead the way Terry had pressed her palm against her busy mouth. The down-toward-the-lake path became a level-beside-the-lake path. Fogel followed it for a while. Then he crouched down on the path until the lake looked much larger to him, as if it were ocean-sized. Again he recited his grandfather's water words. He peered out over the lake, turning his head from left to right and then to left again where the Plaza Hotel reflection swayed upon the water. Would he see a Jewish baby floating like a Moses across the Plaza reflection? No! No more Jewish babies for Fogel. Fogel's own Jew-seed will die, swallowed up by the ocean of America. All he could see on the lake were ducks, a führer in front with his followers faithfully swimming along behind.

Fogel stepped off the pathway and walked down toward the water. He knelt, careful not to get the knees of his lecture suit dirty, and leaned over the edge of the lake. Out of his pocket he took the pigeon feather. He brushed it back and forth over his forehead and then lightly tapped it against both the temple-headache place and the brow-headache place. Then, gently, he set it afloat on the lake. The only blessing he said was: "Go!"

Once Steven had pointed to a pigeon strutting in the supermarket parking lot while he and Fogel were wheeling

116

a grocery wagon to the car. "Look! On the neck! Different colors!" Colors. This gives pleasure to a child. Created at the time of creation: colors.

In the vision of God, Fogel and Terry and Lillian are nothing but a collection of colors, a technicolor movie.

STEVEN TOO. In California, the car is night-blue, the freeway black and gold—Japanese colors, gleaming encompassing colors, whirling around Steven as he drives.

Sharp light comes shooting across the freeway. Fierce noises ride with it. A double-rig is speeding by. Another double-rig is roaring behind it, pursuing it like an army seeking vengeance, trying to gun directly alongside it, straining to overtake it.

Another truck passes, loud as an airplane. Hear, O Steven! You have had colors. Now you have sounds too.

Steven imitates the truck engine, vibrating his tongue against the roof of his mouth for a moment, gunning. Then he listens again. Truck sounds. Tire sounds.

Truck-roar surrounds Steven. Sound presses against him. Sound is outside him. Now it's filling him. It's everywhere, inside, outside, as powerful as color.

Even small sounds, the sound of pages turning.

Yin Yang Jerusalem: Becoming a New Age Jew, $7.95, Papa Bach's Bookstore, Santa Monica Boulevard.

$7.95 even though Steven has said: Why should I be a Jew? To worship a killer God? God is a shit!

Listen to Me, Steven. As a wise man once said: For God all things are fair and good and just, but men have taken some things as just, others as unjust. Source: Heraclitus, Fragment 43.

Yin Yang Jerusalem, Chapter One: Learning About God. Having put off his shoes from his feet, and his socks, and the rest of his clothes, Steven is naked. Having pulled down the living-room shades in his apartment to ensure a restful environment, Steven is in darkness. By TV-screen light, he reads the instructions. All is as it should be: a murder, a car chase, squealing brakes, gunshots, a blond shrieking, a slap; beer pours, foam spills over the rim of a beer glass. Steven walks into the bathroom. On goes the shower, full, hot, loud. Into the kitchen. Soon there too waters pour forth, as if the rock had been struck.

Now roaring. The apartment comes equipped with a blender: mix, mash, blend, puree. And an old Electrolux. Sometimes it doesn't work, but this time it works; it sits on the carpeting, roaring like a young lion. The instructions call for a record of animal sounds: whales singing, dolphins chattering, birds awakening, if possible. It's not possible. Steven riffs along the record shelf until he finds his copy of the ARP Synthesizer Demonstration Record.

Now the mantra. Hear, hear, hear, O Israel, God is one. Silently, Steven repeats it twelve times. He holds the book up in front of the flickering TV set and reads: "While repeating the mantra, listen to the sound of your own heartbeat and breathing. Think of all the sounds you hear, including the sound of silence." The TV set speaks. The stereo makes synthesizer sounds. The heart beats. The telephone rings.

Try spelling out the sounds you hear. Try spelling them in English letters. Impossible! Try spelling them in Hebrew letters. Equally impossible! Analyze the sounds and try inventing an alphabet with which to write them down. Invent new letters to represent new sounds. This is difficult, but it can be done. Here's a hint: To represent one of the sounds, invent a letter which is as different from E as E is from F. Can you do it? When you've finished, you will have invented a new alphabet to write down

118

a new language. But remember, all of these alphabets and languages have already been invented by God.

The telephone rings again, the sound cutting over the voices on the TV set and the roaring of the vacuum cleaner. A message from the Lord? Let it ring. If God wants it to be answered, it will keep on ringing, more than six rings, the minimum recommended by the telephone company, more than seven rings, more than eight, even nine, ten. Is it an emergency? Has Fogel died?

"Hello."

"Steven, hello." No, Fogel is still alive. He's calling.

"Hang on a minute. I'll shut off the TV so I can hear you." And the vacuum cleaner, the blender, the stereo, the shower, the kitchen faucet.

"Steven, I'm doing acupuncture for my headaches."

"Nice."

"They stick a needle in the elbow, it makes the head feel better, and you know what?"

"What?"

"It doesn't even hurt the elbow. Ch'i energy."

"I've heard of it."

"The toe for the kidneys. The heel for the sinuses. For sexual strength also. I work only on the head."

"Is it working?"

"No, but I go on. What good not to keep trying? I don't expect results so quickly. This you learn as you get older. Rome wasn't built in a day. Your career, your studies, are they going so fast? No, it takes time, but you keep on studying, shooting all the pictures. It requires hundreds of pictures to make a movie, correct? Frames." Fogel stopped to catch his breath. "Steven, have I ever interfered with your personal life?"

There was a silence. Then Steven answered: "No."

119

"Steven, now I want to interfere, now I want to tell you. I want to say this: Have children. Soon! Make Jews. Now is the time. Hurry! Children." Fogel waited for a response. Then he waited a little longer. "Do you have a girl?"

"I have lots of girls."

"Do you have a special girl now? A particular girl?"

"Well"—there was another silence—"I see a girl named Elissa from time to time. She works at the school."

"Don't tell me her name. I don't want to know her name. You know what I want to know, only one thing. This: Is she a Jewish girl?"

This was a conversation full of silences. They were especially noticeable without the sound of the vacuum cleaner and the blender, the TV set, the stereo and the shower. "No," Steven finally said, "a Buddhist girl."

"I am not surprised."

Telephone-wire humming: another sound.

"Steven!" Fogel's voice was shaky. "Steven, promise me one thing. Jewish children. Will you promise?"

"I promise to try."

"Not try! Do! Trying is no promise. Results, not attempts. This is what I want. Haven't I always given you? Haven't I always loved you?" Loved, kissed, tickled, squeezed, played soldier with, played gin rummy with, also Monopoly in the little-boy years. Loved, also heart-to-heart talked with, also enjoyed, also admired, sometimes envied even, now in the many-girlfriend years.

"How can I promise? I'd love to promise. I know you want Jews for grandchildren." Now Steven's voice was shaking too. "I want to make you a promise. But how can I make promises for my children? They'll lead their own lives. You know that. You need me to say 'I promise,' but how can I guarantee what somebody else is going to do?"

"Promise!"

"OK, I promise." Steven felt chilly. He crossed his legs. He held the phone tight. His head was hanging down. Surprise! He felt a tear drop onto his thigh. And he didn't even know he was crying.

"Steven, can I believe you? I don't know can I believe you. But Steven, not just one baby or two babies. I stopped too soon with your mother, a mistake. Four babies. Many babies. Jews. Why not eight babies? Why not ten?"

Another silence. Aleph, a silent letter, the first letter of the Hebrew alphabet. "Good-bye," Fogel said. "I have given you my message. Now I put your mother on the telephone."

"Now Chinese doctors. Needles." Lillian's voice trailed hopelessness across the continent. "All the time something else. I buy thirty-five dollars worth of vitamins—B-6, B-12, pantothenic acid, magnesium. You name it, I buy it. And none of it does any good." Lillian was crying. That was another sound. "Nothing works for him. Nothing. Not the vitamins. Not the psychiatrist. Not the needles."

XI

"What are you doing? Now what are you up to?" Light from the upstairs hallway showed Fogel sitting in the shadowy bedroom, posed cross-legged on the rug, Yoga-style.

"I am taking an air bath."

"Stark naked?"

"I have been assured: This is good for my health."

"What are you, a kid? You'll catch cold. You want to know how to cure your headaches? Go to Boston! Get to know Teddy better! That's how to cure your headaches."

But now Fogel was sitting, fully clothed, in Dr. Wax's office among the members of his group. "Always, Dr. Wax, you tell me angry. Angry from my daughter! Angry from my son-in-law! Therefore I have headaches. When you say this, Dr. Wax, that is when I become angry." Did Fogel sound angry? No, Fogel sounded calm, he sounded controlled, not neurotic. "You say: Visit, visit. Talk, talk. Accept, accept. I accept and still I have headaches. God is punishing me."

"I thought you didn't believe in God." Dr. Wax suppressed a smile, as he did whenever he discovered a patient tangled in what he called "neurotic contradiction." "I thought you were a rationalist."

"Correct. I am a rationalist. There is no God. But I have already tried rational headache cures—medical examination, brain scan, psychotherapy. I even count psychotherapy, Dr. Wax. Some people consider it rational." Fogel allowed himself to smile. Why should he suppress smiling at Dr. Wax merely because Dr. Wax suppresses smiling at him? Does Dr. Wax pay Fogel? No, Fogel pays Dr. Wax. "Rational cures do not work. But do I give up? No, I keep on trying. That is how survivors survive. So now it is time for irrationality. Why not religion? Come!" Fogel pointed at Dr. Wax. "Come! We are Jews, children of Israel. Do we visit the synagogue? Do we recite psalms? Maybe such irrationality will help."

"I was under the impression that you had no religion." Dr. Wax had already made this point, Dr. Wax was getting stale. But suddenly Dr. Wax unstaled: "Is there something that's making you frightened, Chaim?"

"Headache!" Dr. Wax has hit his target. Of course frightened. "Headache is frightening me." At the word "headache": an explosion, a dive-bomb, a sudden forehead-attack. Fogel shut his eyes, blocking his view of Dr. Wax, blocking his view of Dr. Wax's diplomas, but not, alas, blocking his headache. Fogel opened his eyes. "Enough headaches and then do you know what happens, Dr. Wax?"

Dr. Wax looked blank; Dr. Wax did not know; Fogel would have to answer the question for him. "Enough headaches and then I die." Was it not his headaches that were making Fogel flicker from north to south and then to north again like a broken compass: first scoffing, then praying; first enlightened, then superstitious? Was it not his headaches that were causing Fogel to flutter this way and that like a match flame about to be extinguished? "Religion equals frightened? Is this not your opinion, Dr. Wax?"

Dr. Wax raised his eyebrows. That was his answer. Insufficient.

"Do you think people pray only when they are frightened?"

"Religion provides comfort for many people."

"Perhaps for you, Dr. Wax. Freud is your religion; Freud, psychosomatic, etcetera, etcetera. This is not my religion. Here is my religion: God is punishing me. But it is no comfort. Come!" Now Fogel pointed at Terry. "Come, come, come!" He jabbed his finger once, twice, three times, pointing at Terry, Terry the pagan who now always looked at Fogel as if he were nothing but a poster on the wall. And what was the proper response to this? The proper response was mum. Mum's the word. Apparently, mum was Terry's desire. A lady's wish, Fogel would respect it, never mentioning his loft visit, never referring to it—no, not even with a wink. Perhaps occasionally with a significant glance. But when one such glance was offered, and then another, Terry refused to see it.

Fogel kept his finger pointed at Terry, but Terry didn't smile. "Come, come!" He wiggled the pointing finger. Still no smile. He pointed at Charlotte with her golden bracelets and shining rings. Had anyone ever suggested that Charlotte might be frightened on the subway because she wore too much jewelry? He pointed at Schwartz who again was sitting with his legs crossed like a girl. "Come, come, come! Is praying any more foolish than this? This psychological therapy?"

Dr. Wax permitted himself to laugh. "And you said you were too enlightened to pray!"

Again Fogel pointed his finger at Dr. Wax. "Histrionic personality disorder. Is this not my diagnosis? You gave it to me, correct?"

Dr. Wax stopped laughing. "Correct," he said.

"I am a hysteric with a histrionic personality disorder." At the foolishness of Dr. Wax's diagnosis, Fogel himself should have laughed. Alas, no laughter came. "I ask you, what is more hysterical than praying?"

For just a moment, Dr. Wax's eyes remained motionless. Then, as if he were about to begin praying himself, he positioned his hands, fingertips together, beneath his chin. "Well, why not pray? It will give the group a chance to interact in a different modality. You'll have to work without me though. I myself don't pray." Dr. Wax moved his hands apart and raised them in the air, palms facing outward. "But you have my blessing."

Dr. Wax was making a joke!

"I DON'T THINK it was a joke," Charlotte insisted. Wearing a small, ribboned hat, she sat in the synagogue on Saturday morning, with Fogel on her left hand, Schwartz on her right. "He doesn't do jokes."

"Of course it was a joke." Schwartz was wearing a red turtleneck shirt and a silver chain. A fringed silken prayer shawl was draped over his shoulders.

He has redeemed us from our enemies. These were the words Fogel heard when he entered the synagogue with Charlotte holding on to his arm and Schwartz and Terry walking in front of him. Annabel was absent, losing weight at a milk farm, but silent Macy walked behind. This was an excursion the group had refused to allow him to avoid. The trees of the forest will sing before God. These were the words Fogel heard when he sat down. When he turned the pages of his prayer book, he heard: Happy is the people whose Lord is God. Around him voices sang: In old age they shall still bear fruit..

"Halleluhu! Halleluhu!" Terry was singing enthusiastically. "I really dig this." She was whispering to Schwartz, but too loud. Too much false smiling! Too much animation! She had not whispered or spoken to Fogel once since the group had gathered in front of the synagogue. "Halleluhu? I thought it was supposed to be hallelujah."

"Sometimes hallelujah also." Fogel leaned across both Charlotte and Schwartz to give Terry his explanation.

Fogel's headache was not enjoying a Sabbath-rest. It was accompanying him to the synagogue, just as he himself as a child had accompanied his grandparents there. "Rise up!" his grandfather used to say to him early in the morning, using the holy language. "Rise up!" And then he would continue in Yiddish: "A visit to the synagogue is the best Sabbath-rest." So Fogel had sat with his grandmother in the women's balcony, counting the pictures of birds on the wall—anything with wings could be considered a bird; also there was a picture of an elephant. He had sat with his grandfather near the ark, among men who smelled of tobacco. He had touched the Torah-scroll with his prayer book and then kissed the book. Fogel's own father had been a rationalist, but rationalism demands sending a child away from the city to spend the summer with his grandparents in a country town. Fogel's grandfather, on the other hand, had been pious. Piety demands: All shall know Him. All shall praise Him. All shall say: There is none like God. Fogel had known, he had praised, he had said. Now again he was praising, he was saying. His head ached.

Terry sang. Charlotte tapped red fingernails on the covers of her prayer book and hummed. Schwartz slowly read the prayers, his tongue stumbling over the Hebrew consonants. Macy, the youngest neurotic, was the product of a pious home. He knew both the words and the melodies. But when

126

the cantor sang, "God reigns, God has reigned, God will reign forever," Macy frowned and muttered, "Bullshit!" and when the congregation sang, "And we will bless God, now and forever, Hallelujah!" Macy said, "Bullshit!" again. Voltaire, Lessing, Gibbon—any rationalist no matter how enlightened—would be offended by such behavior in such a place. Hastily, Fogel tugged at Macy's sleeve. "Shh! Shh! Not nice!"

Macy jerked back his head and raised his left hand, jabbing the air with his middle finger. Giving the finger, this is called in English: a sign of disrespect. Foolish laughter spilled from Terry's mouth. But suddenly she looked toward the front of the synagogue and became serious: The curtain of the ark was being drawn open, exposing the holy Torah-scrolls to view. Fogel jumped up. Slowly, Macy stood up too. Everywhere around the neurotics, Jews rose and started singing again, deep-voiced and confident, proclaiming: "His glory is over the earth and the heaven." Fogel reached across to nudge Terry. "Hallelujah. This time you hear it. Hallelujah."

Men, carrying a Torah-scroll, formed a procession and moved down from the ark-platform to march among the Jews. Children ran down the aisle toward the front of the synagogue and reached up to touch the Torah. Without thinking, Fogel squeezed past Charlotte and Schwartz, past Terry, out into the aisle himself, hurrying to the front of the synagogue. With the silken fringes of his prayer shawl held in his fingers, he reached over to touch the velvet covering of the scroll. He brought his fingers to his lips: a kiss. As he edged back into his seat again, Schwartz patted him on the back, Charlotte squeezed his arm, even Terry seemed to smile; but Macy hissed at Fogel and then whispered, "Coward!"

Let Macy hiss! How can the opinion of such a youth matter? Isn't every one of Dr. Wax's neurotics a coward?

"I think Macy should go back to the synagogue," Charlotte declared when the group was assembled again in Dr. Wax's office for its Tuesday meeting. "You should have seen how much good it did him!" Charlotte grasped Macy's hand and squeezed it. "It really brought out his feelings. I've never seen him respond so much to anything before."

Macy pulled his hand away. "You won't get me back there. I finished religion. I already had too much."

"Chaim changed his thinking and got religion. Maybe you will too." Dr. Wax glanced at Fogel to see his reaction. There was none to see. Therefore Dr. Wax looked over to see Macy's reaction.

"No way!" Macy drummed a finger against his thigh, the very same finger he had used to gesture vulgarly in the synagogue. "I'm not like Chaim. I already told you, I finished with religion. Chaim didn't finish with religion yet."

"Is that true, Chaim?"

"It is true." Never mind hissings! Never mind intellectual integrity. "It is true. Absolutely." Could merely one synagogue visit be enough to cure headaches? "True," Fogel said again firmly—firmly, decisively, because in Dr. Wax's office indecision invited lengthy group discussions. "I have not finished visiting the synagogue. One more time with the Torah-scrolls. This time a weekday. No Sabbath crowds. I am going back. Definitely true."

"Maybe you'll think it over too then, Macy." Dr. Wax always labored assiduously to uncover any neurotic contradictions that might be lurking among his clientele. "Why don't you go along too?"

Macy refused to answer, though Charlotte reached for his

hand again and held it. The group waited in silence for Macy to speak. This was a traditional group technique: Break stubbornness with lengthy silence. Normally, the silence would continue until Macy finally answered or until Dr. Wax chose to speak. But Terry shattered the tradition by answering instead. "I'm going back."

With her chin raised defiantly, Terry glared at Fogel. "Not to keep *him* company."

Again Terry acknowledges Fogel's presence! Again Terry looks at Fogel, even if angrily! Again in Terry's eyes, Fogel is a person, not merely a wall decoration!

"I have my own reasons for going." Terry stopped short, establishing another silence, a silence which nobody interrupted. "I'm going because ..." Terry stopped again. "Because," she finally said, "because maybe God will touch me."

Ah, if Fogel had only kept his pigeon feather instead of sending it off to sail away on the beautiful water.

Schwartz began clapping his hands—loud flat smacks, applause in Fogel's honor. "You really found out how to turn her on, Chaim. I have to hand it to you."

"He doesn't know how to turn me on." Blushing, Terry moved her head fast to keep Fogel from looking at her, but as she did, she glanced at him angrily. Certainly, this was a look filled with emotion! "And you ..." Now she was looking at Schwartz. "You don't know how to turn me on either."

"When will you teach me how, baby?" Schwartz blew Terry a kiss. "I never figured you for a nun. Hallelujah!"

Impatiently, Dr. Wax waved his hand at Schwartz, a shut-up gesture. Schwartz shut up.

It was time for group seriousness. "Why do you want to go to the synagogue, Terry?" Charlotte asked solemnly.

129

"Because I want to get healed," Terry said quietly. Suddenly her hand shot up in the air and she thumbed her nose at Dr. Wax. "Imaginary cancer, my ass!"

Dr. Wax was accustomed to Terry's contempt. No expression showed in his eyes.

Terry lowered her hand to her lap. "I don't believe in Dr. Wax like you do!" She stared at her hand. "You think he's God! If I want God, I'll go direct to the source. I don't need his kind of therapy. I hate it here."

"She hates us!" Schwartz gasped, covering up his face with his hands. He was pretending to be in pain.

"I don't hate the group. I like you, even . . ." Terry flicked her hand toward Fogel. "Even this one."

This one! This one was Chaim Fogel. So, Terry now admits it: She likes Chaim Fogel.

And here was proof: Despite angry talk, despite angry looks, Terry was willing to accompany him to the synagogue again.

"COME! Again we will try Jewish superstitions. Maybe this time they will work." Outside the West Fourth Street station, Fogel attempted to hand Terry a subway token. "I have done your superstitions, witches, needles, pantothenic acid. Now you do mine."

Terry refused to take the token. Instead, she stuck out her tongue. At Dr. Wax, she thumbs her nose. At Fogel, she sticks out her tongue—this tongue Fogel remembers. Doesn't he also have a tongue, a tongue with a different history? But then Terry stuck in her tongue and reached into the woven bag she always carried, a Mexican-looking woolen sack, to take out her own subway token.

"A superstitious age," Fogel shouted over the noise of the

subway car. "Even though supposedly an age of science."
These words might help Terry understand this: Unlike
Schwartz, unlike horny-rims, Fogel was interested in Terry's
mind, not just in her body. The car rocked. Fogel grasped
Terry's arm, the fleshiest part, but Terry moved away. "I
myself am no longer immune to superstition," Fogel said.
Terry shrugged. This did not neccessarily mean: I don't care.
It could mean merely: I can't hear you.

Screaming, the subway stopped at Times Square. Again
putting his hand on Terry's arm, but this time very lightly,
Fogel steered her up dirty cement steps out into air that was
as fetid as the subway-station air. "I will take you downtown
again in a taxi. This I promise. Here it is no good." Fogel
pretended to spit. "Even if they planted trees, still no good."
Walking south on Seventh Avenue, among human vermin,
all colors, he patted Terry's arm. "A girl in this environment." Terry moved away slightly. "Alone on the subway.
Not right. Dangerous."

On the heavy wooden door of the Needle Trades Synagogue a sign said: *We Are Always Open.* Nobody was inside.
With Terry behind him—why bother arm-holding if arm-
holding was not desired?—Fogel walked slowly to the front
of the dimly lit room and then up onto the platform to stand
before the curtained ark. Terry sat down in a front-row pew.

"Dr. Wax should be here to pray with us." Fogel reached
out to touch the ark curtain. It was made of velvet embroidered with golden lions, their claws unsheathed ready to
attack.

"Dr. Wax doesn't pray." One of Terry's bad habits was
this: In religious edifices she spoke too loud.

"This is something you don't know."

"He said so."

"To you, perhaps, but not to me." Fogel raised one edge of the ark curtain and peeked in. There they were, the Torah-scrolls.

"You were right there when he said it." Not merely loud, but forceful, also not ladylike. "He said it to the group."

Carefully, with the index finger of his right hand, Fogel touched one of the scrolls. "Siseleh, miseleh," he whispered. This was what his grandmother had said after one of his baby teeth fell out when he was spending the summer in her wooden house in Stoianov. "Siseleh, miseleh." She had stood over the cookstove-fire and dropped in the tooth. "This bone is dead," she called out. "Give the little one a strong bone in its place." And then, three times, she traced a circle with her finger over the fire.

Her bones were burned. Her husband's bones, her children's bones, her grandchildren's—burned in the fire. Slowly, Fogel drew three circles on the Torah. Then he touched his finger to the center of his forehead where pain was burning. He let the ark curtain fall shut again.

"Now you."

Terry held back for a minute. Then she stood up and slowly ascended the platform. And then, as she reached over to open the ark curtain, she squealed with pleasure. "Siseleh, miseleh," she said. "Pauline would love this."

"Wait!" Fogel grabbed her hand. "Can a woman touch?"

"Don't be disgusting!" Terry jerked her hand away and tugged at the drawstring to open the ark. Three Torah-scrolls were revealed, standing like judges. In each of them was written many times the word "wicked."

Fogel turned toward her solemnly. "Are you unclean now?"

"What do you mean unclean? What are you talking about?"

Fogel pressed his lips shut and raised his eyebrows. Slowly, he waved his hand from side to side.

"Oh my God!" Terry reached down, around Fogel's back, and pinched him hard on the portion of his body that in the holy tongue is called "the beneath," the portion which now, as was proper, faced away from the open ark. "No wonder you have headaches!"

A woman clean, a woman unclean—to Terry what did that matter? Terry turned back toward the ark and slowly ran a fingernail along the nap of a velvet Torah cover. Then, in a loud voice, she solemnly repeated the magic formula. "Siseleh! Miseleh! Siseleh! Miseleh! Siseleh! Miseleh!" Each word echoed in the hollow synagogue chamber. The room began to tremble. "Siseleh! Miseleh! Siseleh! Miseleh!" A subway train was rolling underneath the holy ark. Now every time Terry called out the word "Siseleh," she drew a circle on the Torah scroll and then drew another circle on her own body, around the nipple of her right breast. With each "Miseleh," she drew a circle on a different Torah-scroll and then another circle on herself, on her left breast. When she finished, she slowly pulled the ark curtain closed. "Lumps," she said softly.

"Me," Fogel whispered. "Also for me."

"You did you. I do me."

"Also ..." Fogel took a deep breath. "Also I will help you."

"No way!" Terry sounded angry again. "Besides, I never did you any good before."

"Me," Fogel said again.

Terry reached for the drawstring and pulled the curtain open. Not always an angry girl. Not always an unfeeling girl. Sometimes, even, an understanding girl. "Siseleh, miseleh," she mumbled. "Siseleh, miseleh." She leaned forward and

133

traced three circles on the middle Torah-scroll. Then turning toward Fogel—did it matter that she stood with her back to the ark?—she quickly drew three more circles on his forehead.

Three scrolls. Three charms. Three circles. Terry leaned forward and kissed each Torah. Three kisses. Then, though she had seemed unconcerned and hurried only a moment before, she kissed the palm of her hand and rested it on Fogel's forehead. "Siseleh, miseleh," she said again, not mumbling this time but slowly and seriously. And then when she took her hand away, she kissed the place where her hand had rested. Finally, she drew the curtain closed.

"It hurts. It still hurts. It hurts. It hurts." God magic, Terry magic, psychiatry magic—nothing worked.

Fogel sat down heavily in the big velvet-covered chair that stood beside the ark and rocked from side to side. "My bones will burn." He rubbed his forehead with his knuckles, he kneaded and pressed and pinched his forehead skin, he held cold hands out toward Terry. Not such a bad girl. Not always. Terry put her arms around his head and pressed his face against her breast. "Hallelujah!" Fogel cried out. "Hallelujah! This they sing." With her hands spread wide, Terry covered his eyes. "Hallelujah!" Fogel cried out again.

The noise of Fogel's Hallelujahs fills the synagogue and flows out onto Seventh Avenue. It mingles with the traffic sounds, with the roar of subway trains underneath the avenue, with the grinding and scraping of trucks driving through the tunnels and along the turnpikes, with the blare of *Jugendkultur* music on truck radios, the chattering of birds, the shouting of crowds, the clicking of typewriters, the papery noises of pages turning. Listen, Steven! Here it is, for the day when you're ready to shoot your next film. Here it is: the sound track—a film entitled *GOD*.

A BLACK MAN drove the taxi taking Terry back to NYU. When she got out of the cab, she squeezed Fogel's hand. Headsick, he weakly squeezed back. The driver took Fogel on three more blocks to his subway stop. The fare was two dollars and fifteen cents. Fogel reached into his pocket and pulled out two dollar bills, and a dime and a nickel. The driver got no tip.

Walking down the steep stairway toward the subway tracks, Fogel held tightly onto his briefcase. It was valuable, containing notes on the town of Wolfenbüttel where Lessing had worked as a librarian for the Duke of Brunswick. What surrounded Lessing? A *Schloss* and stone churches, a library and half-timbered houses, grassy promenades for strolling and—a day's coach-drive away—the Lüneburger Heath for philosophical rambles.

Certainly Wolfenbüttel was more tranquil than New York. Certainly other centuries were better than the twentieth. Fogel's subway car was crowded, Fogel's subway windows dirty. In one of the windows he could see his own reflection, dead-faced, dust. History was flashing by him, swift as a train, each fact bright, like the tunnel-lights shining outside the subway-car windows. In the blackness around each of the lights there was one fact: death. Powerful and electric, pain rushed through Fogel's head. It lurched to a stop. It screamed forward. His right leg was trembling. He set his briefcase on the train floor between his legs and pressed his right leg against it, but the trembling wouldn't stop.

Why was he trembling? Was this the day of his death? Was this the day chosen for the death of the Jews? Was this the day when God's experiment ends, the day when the Torah-scrolls fall down within their cupboards, the day of the final solution, the day the black Hebrew letters fly off in different directions, only one letter left, the last—Tav, the

135

brand of judgment? Fogel could feel it burning on his forehead; his eyes were smarting. It was on the forehead of Lillian, his wife, of Steven, his son. It was branded all over his
daughter's body. God had set it there, on her nipples, on her
belly where the child was rising, on her thighs, on her upper
lip and her lower lip; she was as if already dead; and now
Fogel could feel subway sweat in the darkness of the tunnel,
running down his forehead, washing away the brand of death.
This meant: Fogel was already dead.

He and all the Jews.

His Lillian was dying.

His daughter was gone.

His son's flesh was melting off its bones.

Rabbi Akiba was flayed alive. Rashi was dead. Moses Mendelssohn was dead.

The heads of the history departments at the following
institutions of higher learning: Brandeis University, Yeshiva
University, Bar Ilan University, Hebrew University in Jerusalem, Jews' College of the University of London, Dropsie
College of Jewish and Cognate Studies—all these were dead
along with their colleagues, their students, the donors who
had paid their salaries, their kosher butchers, their rabbis,
the circumcisers who had circumcised their sons, the members of the Jewish Chautauqua Society who had listened to
their lectures. The men of B'nai B'rith were dead, the women
of Hadassah, the entire membership of the Bergen-Belsen
Memorial Foundation, all the members of the Jewish Publication Society, all the subscribers to the Jewish Book Club,
all the members of the United Synagogue of America. All
the Jews in the land of Israel, religious or not, kibbutz members and nonkibbutz members, Oriental or Western—all
dead. While Fogel was hiding in the darkness of the tunnel
between Fourteenth Street and Forty-second Street, with the

mark of death on his forehead, enemies had encompassed Israel about; they came with the sword, the gun, the bomb; the great fire came down out of heaven; the Angel of Death passed among them; no one was spared, no child, no little Fogel; all were killed; all lay dead. All the Jews in this country, in that: the Jews in Argentina, the Jews in America, the Jews in Curaçao, the oldest Jewish settlement in the New World, the Jews in Germany, the Jews in Italy—all dead. God made them, God now had finished with them. If not today, then in a hundred years. It stood to reason. In a hundred years every member of Hadassah—Lillian, even Lillian—every one of them would be dead. Inside Fogel's head there was clawing, screaming. Inside his head or outside? Perhaps it was the scream of the subway wheels. In the midst of this screaming, a quick silence on the train. Everyone was staring at him.

Shuddering, the train stopped. Forty-second Street. Fogel was pushed out. He pushed himself out, out of this tunnel, this journey, into another tunnel, another journey, to White Plains. But in this station, was he the only Jew walking among the crowds? When he got to White Plains, would he find that the Angel had entered his house, that his wife was lying on the kitchen floor or slumped on the sofa or fallen on the walkway leading out to the garage? A Jew, therefore dead. Gripping his black briefcase, Fogel walked onto the dimly lit platform of Track 21. There was his train, one of the new ones, a train with sealed windows.

Inside, at a window seat beside two other men, his friend Broitman was sitting! Then another Jew was still alive! Fogel's leg began trembling again, his fingers turned weak, his briefcase almost fell out of his hand. "Hallo, Fogel!" Broitman called out cheerfully. In his hand was a dead cigar. He waved it at Fogel. "No seat. No seat."

Fogel stopped in the aisle for a moment and looked through Broitman as if he weren't there. Another Jew alive, another survivor. Then, without even nodding recognition, he walked past. Let Broitman think this: Fogel is embarrassed and ashamed because his daughter has married a black man. As if ashamed were the word. As if embarrassed were the word. No. The word was afraid.

XII

It hurts," Fogel whispered to Lillian. "I'll die. Drilling! Would it hurt like this unless I'm going to die?"

Lillian edged away from him in the bed. "First you run away from the Russians and the Polacks. Now you're running away from Negroes."

"Blacks. The proper word is blacks."

"Marlene shouldn't be traveling to see us. We should travel, not her." Lillian patted her pillow. "I wonder how big she is."

"Let her be the one who does the traveling. I have headaches."

Headaches! Yes, indeed! Driving two hundred miles, getting off the turnpike at the right exit, finding Commonwealth Avenue, Brighton, parking in the slush next to a snowbank, climbing up to the third floor—to what? A black man's walk-up.

"Poppa!" Teddy grabbed Fogel's hand. "Welcome! Welcome!"

"Hello. Hello." Fogel's handshake was weak.

Lillian kissed Teddy's cheek and hugged him.

He enthusiastically hugged back. "How you doin', Momma? Ain't that my baby!"

Before did Teddy have such a pronounced Negro accent?

"A lovely apartment!" Lillian peered over Teddy's shoulder. "Lovely!" It was late afternoon. Sunlight shone into the room, onto a white wicker rocking chair and a glossy white table. There was a woven rug on the floor, pale blue and white; another rug, its twin, hung on the wall. Beneath the hanging rug there was a white wicker sofa with red cushions on it. Red, white and blue—America. Throw out the red cushions and what do you have? The national colors of the reborn Jewish state.

"Where is my daughter?" Even to himself, Fogel sounded angry. He himself had to admit it. So he waved his hand at an immense, almost tree-sized philodendron standing in the corner and placatingly added, "Nice."

"She had to do some shopping. She'll be back in a little while."

Fogel sat down on the sofa.

"I'm going to look at the apartment." Lillian had adopted the high, happy voice she was accustomed to use whenever she talked about babies or weddings. "Spanish!" she called out from the bedroom. "A lovely set! But no curtains. Hasn't Marlene picked them out yet."

"Nobody can look in." Though there was absolutely no suggestiveness in Teddy's voice, Fogel felt his face getting red. A bedroom without curtains!

"Chaim!" Now Lillian was in the kitchen. "Chaim, refinished oak!"

"Hey, let me get you something to drink." Standing next to the sofa, Teddy looked taller than Fogel had remembered. Can an already-married man still be growing?

"I could have a little schnapps."

Teddy's nose wrinkled. Does he understand? This one's a stickler. What's Schnapps? Is it that new liqueur being advertised in *The New Yorker*? Maybe it's a Jewish beverage. "I've got scotch or Canadian." Teddy smiled bravely. "What

140

is this stuff anyway? Schweppes, Schnapps, a kind of gin?"

Fogel answered only, "Canadian."

"On the rocks? Or with something? I've got some soda." Teddy stopped smiling, as if he had suddenly become exhausted. "I think there's some ginger ale around."

"Just a shot glass."

"A little glass of schnapps. That's what you need." Lillian emerged from the bedroom. "Then you'll have the strength to look around the house. You'll love it. Ted's study, his books. It's going to be the baby's room." She turned to Teddy apologetically. "It was a long drive."

Teddy hurried into the kitchen and began probing under the sink for the bottle of Canadian Club.

"Knowledge," the rabbi had said in his velvety voice the evening Marlene took Teddy to the synagogue to visit the conversion class. No commitment, don't worry, nothing to be scared of, just exploratory, just to see what it's like— these were Marlene's words. "Knowledge is the hallmark of the Jewish people." Now Teddy had knowledge: Schnapps is the Hebrew word for Canadian. But there's knowledge and there's knowledge. "What good is a Ph.D.?" Teddy had said as he unlocked the apartment door after the synagogue visit. "What good is it if you can't even pronounce your father-in-law's name?"

Marlene took off her coat and stationed herself in front of Teddy. "Chaim," she said. "Come on, Teddy, say it! Chaim."

Teddy tried.

"Chaim," Marlene said again. *"Chhh!"*

Again Teddy tried.

"No." Marlene reached up and loosened Teddy's necktie. "That isn't quite it. Too much H, not enough CH. A little more weight on the guttural. *Chhh!"*

Teddy took his jacket off. "Chaim," he said. "CHHH."

"Again," Marlene called out. "From the throat. Again."

"Chaim. *Chhh!* Chaim."

"That's it!" Marlene shouted. "Chaim!"

Teddy tried it again: "Chaim." This time too it came out right.

Marlene grasped Teddy's hand and shook it. "By God, you've got it! You've really got it!" She slid one foot forward: a tango movement. "The rain in Chelm," she sang out. "The rain in Chelm falls mainly on the Chaims." Teddy stretched out his right arm; he put his left arm around Marlene's shoulder. Together they began to tango around the room. "The rain in Chelm," Teddy sang. "I've really got it! The rain in Chelm falls mainly on the Chaims."

L'Chaim! A toast! To Teddy! Teddy, stop worrying! A brother doesn't jeopardize his black identity just by becoming a Jew.

Again Teddy says it. Chaim. This time he's in the synagogue again, with the book held in his hand and Marlene whispering the word. Marlene's finger moves over the page to point to another word in the Hebrew text, to show its translation: Baruch. Blessed.

Teddy mouths the word: Baruch. There's another CH for you. He whispers it so Marlene can hear him.

Marlene isn't the only one who hears. The God of Abraham, the God of Isaac, the God of Jacob hears too.

Seated near the back in the big synagogue on Commonwealth Avenue, a few blocks away from the apartment, Teddy says the word again. Baruch. He searches his book and finds the word twice, its black letters twisted, hunched in line, poised as if for flight. He points to the letters, showing Marlene. Her eyes glow like ovens. She closes her own book and sets it down; now she holds on to one side of Teddy's book.

The congregation rises. Teddy rises. The congregation is seated. Teddy is seated. "One more strike," Teddy whispers to Marlene. "One more strike and I'm out."

"L'CHAIM!" Fogel raised the shot glass of Canadian and downed it in one gulp. Did it make him feel any better? No. His head still hurt.

"I'll show you around Boston tomorrow." Teddy held out the bottle toward Fogel, offering a refill. "You get into my car and I'll show you everything: Harvard, Bunker Hill, the Paul Revere House. I'll take you to the Gardner Museum. You ever been to the Gardner Museum?"

Smiling, Lillian looked over at Fogel, but he gave no response. Her smile drooped. Teddy put the bottle down on the floor next to Fogel's feet. "If you want to get out of the city, we can go to Plymouth. Plymouth Rock. Or maybe off in the other direction, up to Salem, Marblehead." He waited for an answer. No answer came. "You know. Salem. The House of Seven Gables."

"What I would really like to see most," Lillian said softly, almost romantically, "is Brandeis University."

For just longer than a moment, Teddy was quiet. Then he said, "Terrific. We'll combine it with a visit to Lexington and Concord."

"We're not staying too long, you know." Fogel reached down to the floor, picked up the bottle and stretched out his arm toward Teddy, a signal for Teddy to take the bottle away. "I don't have a class Monday, but I should get back anyway."

"Suit yourself." Teddy set the bottle on the end table next to the sofa. His face looked older suddenly, African and thin. Marlene's key could be heard in the door.

"What are you doing carrying?" Lillian screamed. "Why

are you lifting packages?" Marlene was almost in her eighth month, but she wasn't that big.

"Hello, Daddy." Marlene set down her grocery bag and ran over to Fogel, who stretched his neck upward making his cheek available to be kissed. Lillian rushed over to embrace Marlene. Then Fogel stood up to hug his daughter too. There they were, the three of them, a tableau: The Fogel Family. Only Steven was required to complete it, but he was miles away in California, and Steven never was much of a hugger anyway. Teddy picked up Marlene's grocery bag and carried it into the kitchen.

"A lovely apartment. You've fixed it up beautifully." Lillian patted Marlene's stomach. "It's good you haven't put on a lot of weight. Look, Chaim!" She gripped Fogel's arm and guided it over so that he could pat too. "This is a Fogel in here."

Fogel patted. He pretended to smile.

"It's OK if you don't get curtains for the bedroom." Lillian winked at Marlene. "Teddy"—Teddy was in the kitchen noisily putting groceries away—"Teddy's going to drive us around sight-seeing tomorrow."

"Your husband is planning to show us Brandeis University." Fogel snorted. "Also two cities, Lexington and Concord."

"Once they asked him to teach there."

"In Lexington? Concord?" Lillian was solemn. "Such historic places!"

"No, at Brandeis."

Fogel's throat narrowed. Who had ever asked Fogel to teach anywhere? Always, he'd been the one to do the applying. And, except for at NYU, not successfully either. He had perished, even though he had published: two papers in *Enlightenment Studies* before the new editor came in—one precociously in the fifties, another satisfactorily in the sixties. Plus a lengthy bibliographical note in the Yearbook of the

Lessing Society. Nevertheless, he had perished—merely an associate professor; they would never promote him to full. The manuscript of *Protodromos Lessing: The First Postreligious Man* was sitting in a closet in White Plains after having spent a year and a half being read, unfavorably, at the University of Toledo Press and over protracted though lesser times, at Yale, Princeton, Oklahoma, the Jewish Publication Society, Michigan, Wayne State, Columbia, Harvard, California, Tulane, Doubleday, Scribner's, Bobbs-Merrill and Random House. Maybe it could be sent out again, maybe to the University of New Mexico Press, maybe to Oxford. Had Teddy even finished his dissertation yet?

And five or six years ago, when Fogel had gone to the American Historical Association meeting at the New York Hilton, there had even been a position open at Brandeis for an eighteenth-century man! And Mirelli of Brandeis, a Gentile, not even the chairman of the department, inspecting Fogel's vita and, seeing under Publications, "Some Thoughts on Influences in Lessing and M. Mendelssohn," *Enlightenment Studies*, XIV: 3, pp. 317-34, had had the nerve to say: "There's room for a good analytical study of Lessing."

"I already wrote it! Years ago! But nobody published it. If it was Rousseau, I'd have to fight them off. Lessing, they don't care."

"Do you teach Lessing?"

"A whole course? Are you crazy? They wouldn't want it, they wouldn't let you, the administration. Even at Harvard there isn't a whole course on Lessing. Nowhere on this side of the Atlantic. Nowhere here! Nowhere!"

Nowhere. This is where Chaim Fogel gets offered new jobs.

"Urban Studies Department." Marlene settled down next to her father on the sofa. "A course on the contemporary person as seen in films, newspapers, black literature and the reports of the FBI. They're published, you know. You should read them. In paperback. Stolen documents."

"But I decided not to go." Teddy walked back into the room and tapped Marlene's knee. "Want a drink?"

"Ginger ale. Nothing alcoholic." Marlene smiled at her mother, a smile only a mother could understand. Then she turned to smile at Teddy. This smile could fit into an advertisement in a women's magazine or into a TV commercial. "He decided," Marlene leaned closer to Fogel, "to stay at BU so he could devote his efforts to black kids who were still in the ghetto rather than spending his time with all Jewish kids at Brandeis."

"If they are Jewish students at Brandeis," Fogel said, stiffening his back, "then they also are in the ghetto." Maybe Teddy was an anti-Semite. His son-in-law not only Gentile, not only black, but an anti-Semite! This was what fate had planned for him. This plus, in his old age, paranoia.

"Lovely," Lillian murmured as Teddy drove his Volvo around the Brandeis campus. Everywhere, among trees which God had planted before the Jews arrived, were sunny buildings planted by the Jews. "So lovely!" Lillian and Marlene were sitting in the backseat. "Pretty as a picture. Which one is the dining hall?" Lillian leaned forward to get a better view. "I always wondered: Do they serve only kosher or is it that they serve also kosher?"

Nobody answered.

Lillian leaned toward Teddy. "I should call your mother to say hello. It doesn't seem right not to call her when we're here in Boston. You'll think I'm terrible, but I'd love to get a recipe from her. Soul food. Where else could I get it?"

"Marlene's mother is an aficionado of international cooking," Fogel explained, staring through the windshield to avoid facing Teddy. He himself would never dare make a remark so

146

openly racist. This is something a person learns teaching at a large urban university. "An aficionada I should say."

"I can give you recipes." Even though he was driving, Teddy turned around toward Lillian, grinning. "I'd make you ham hocks for supper tonight but . . ." His face turned serious. "It's late for that." He added a housewifely warning. "You always have to start cookin' your ham hocks early."

"Cut it out, Teddy!" Marlene snapped her fingers on the back of Teddy's head, then turned to her mother. "He ought to make you baked beans." She cupped one hand at the side of her mouth. "His family's been in Boston since the seventeen hundreds."

"How 'bout some Colonel What's-his-name Kaintucka Frahd Chicken?" Teddy said. "You lak dat?"

Lillian pointed at a building they were passing. "I like to think that we paid for that very window over there."

"The Fogel Memorial Window." Fogel rubbed his thumb against his forehead. "Every year Marlene's mother spends a week on the telephone raising money for Brandeis University."

Even though there was still snow on the ground, Lillian opened her window a crack for a breath of real Brandeis air. "I never had dormitories at Hunter College. I never had campus life."

"I had dormitories," Fogel said. "I had dormitories plenty."

This kept everyone silent until the Volvo had passed out of the campus gates.

Finally, after they had seen Lexington, after they had seen Concord, after Fogel had curtly said, "No! No Harvard!" when Teddy had offered to show them Harvard, Fogel called out, "Howard Johnson's! Howard Johnson's!" He had seen a sign along the road.

"My father gets hungry." Marlene put her hand on Ted-

147

dy's shoulder. This was a wifely signal: Stop the car.

"When he gets hungry," Lillian said softly, as if she were speaking about somebody who had just died, "he gets grumpy."

"When I get hungry, it aggravates my headaches."

But what didn't aggravate Fogel's headaches? Back at the apartment, when Marlene announced the names chosen for the baby—Eli Garrison Jessep, if a boy, after Fogel's dead grandfather; Bryna Garrison Jessep, if a girl, after Fogel's dead grandmother—Fogel's headache attacked again, behind the left eye.

"Lovely." Lillian pronounced her blessing. "Why Garrison? Just like Teddy's middle name. What an unusual name!"

"In Teddy's family, every baby is named Garrison."

"Why is that?"

"Because," Teddy said, "Garrison was the Moses of the shvartzers."

Marlene laughed. Lillian blushed. Fogel's eyes widened.

"Excuse me," Teddy said. "Not the Moses, the Aaron."

Marlene turned her head very slowly to stare at her mother. "Garrison the abolitionist. Remember?"

Lillian nodded as if she did remember.

"Every baby," Teddy said. "Every baby. My great-great-uh-great-grandmother went up to Garrison's office, *The Liberator* office, right, that was his paper, on Tremont Street here, and she asked to see Garrison and she pointed to her belly—she was pregnant. 'Every baby out of this,' she told him, 'every baby's going to be named Garrison.' "

"What an interesting family!" Lillian reached over to take Marlene's hand. "How old is it?"

Teddy bowed his head toward Fogel. "Just as old as yours."

Wrong! Mankind may have originated in Africa, but surely

148

the Fogel family antedated the Jesseps. In his grandfather's synagogue, Fogel had seen records, all destroyed now, burned like the synagogue and the Jews themselves. Not only an ancient family, in Stoianov by the sixteenth century, but even a distinguished family. There were rabbis, there were authors of books. And furthermore was not Fogel also related on his mother's side, though through marriage only, to the eminent historian Meir Balaban, author of *Zydzi Lwowcsy na Przeliomie XVI go is XVII Wieku* and of *Yidn in Poylen*? An important scholar, though by no means concerned, like Fogel himself, with the mainstream of world history. Ah, what sufferings Balaban had written of, what torments.

What headaches! With his fingertips, Fogel lightly touched his forehead.

.

"LET'S YOU and I go for a drive." Marlene walked over to the closet, pulled out her father's overcoat and handed it to him. "I want to show you certain things in Boston. Where Benjamin Franklin went to school."

"Harvard University!" Lillian stood up and clapped her hands. "We really ought to see it."

"Franklin didn't go to the university." Fogel was indignant. "It wasn't a university, even in Europe the universities weren't worthy of the name." He sat with the heavy coat on his lap. "Eighteenth-century intellectual life went on outside the universities." He stretched out his legs, causing the coat to slide onto the floor. He turned to Teddy, as if Teddy might understand. "Unlike the twentieth," he said, nodding sagely. "Unlike the twentieth."

"Where Franklin went to school when he was a boy, I mean." Marlene got her own coat and put it on. Even with all the buttons closed, it still fit her. "Just you and I," she

149

said to Fogel. "I'll do the driving. Pick up your coat. Let's go." When Marlene was a child of eleven or twelve, just before she became a woman, she would come into the living room where Fogel was reading his journals, keeping up with the field, and with her hand on her hip sing him a song, a torch song: "I want to be loved by you and only by you." Fogel would smile and applaud and ask her to sing it again, but then Marlene would get embarrassed and run from the room.

"Put your coat on." Lillian bent down to pick up Fogel's coat. "Let her drive. You do sight-seeing. You relax. You sit back."

What father can sit back and relax while his daughter drives?

"That's where it is." Marlene pointed to a red brick building. "Franklin's school." She stopped the car. In the argument over driving, she had prevailed.

The building was in mock-eighteenth-century style, built maybe in 1920, maybe in 1930. "Franklin didn't go to school here," Fogel said tolerantly. What did his daughter know of architecture? Urban affairs, yes. Architectural history, no. "There would be a plaque on the building. Is there a plaque?"

"No, not in this building, in this school," Marlene said impatiently. She looked directly into Fogel's eyes. "Teddy went here too. In this building. Do you like it?" Three boys walked out of the school's front door. They were white.

"Very fine."

"I hoped you'd like it." Marlene started the car again. "And Teddy too."

"To be frank," Fogel said, "Jewish, I'd like him just fine. Black, frankly, I don't care for him so much. So what if I was almost mugged by a black man on Central Park South. You don't hear all the news from White Plains. So what, it isn't prejudice, my reasoning. How could I be prejudiced, also a victim?" They were turning corners, they were passing churches, trolley tracks, stores, soon tenements, a railroad bridge. "I don't feel prejudiced against Negroes per se, what's it to me, a European, remember. To have my children wiped out, this I'm prejudiced against." Fogel exhaled heavily. "This is my headache."

"What are you talking about?" Marlene stared straight ahead, at the street traffic. "Am I wiped out?" She took her right hand off the steering wheel and shook it in the air to demonstrate. "I'm right here. I'm not wiped out. I'm here. You are prejudiced!" She slapped her hand down on the dashboard.

"Jew!" Fogel roared. "Jude! Yiddishkeit! Sh'ma Yisrael! This is what I'm talking about." Now, on the sidewalks, only black faces could be seen. "To me, Teddy is Hitler."

Marlene pulled the car over to the curb and shifted into park. She turned off the motor and leaned her head on the steering wheel. Would she cry? Her face was invisible. "I was going to take you to see the house where Teddy grew up. Where his parents live." Her voice was choked.

"Take me, take me, I want to see. You think I'm a monster? Eichmann?" Marlene didn't move. "I will drive. You show me." Fogel looked around dubiously. An enormous, groaning trailer truck was rumbling by. "Even in these streets." They had been driving through a section of Boston which hadn't been plowed conscientiously. The snow had turned to ice.

Marlene sat up straight and wiped her cheek—not a tear wipe, just a cheek wipe. She started the car. "I'll drive."

"Drive."

But it was too silent. They went under an elevated railroad line. No trains went by. "I am not a monster," Fogel whispered. "You think your father is a cruel man, a warrior?"

Now they were driving alongside a large park. Fogel pointed at it. "Pretty."

"It's not safe anymore. It used to be safe. Now Teddy's mother won't set foot in it."

"Maybe it's white muggers. There are white muggers. This they should write in the newspapers, as a reminder, to improve race relations." Wasn't it true? Hadn't people been robbed by whites, beaten up, murdered? It wasn't just in Europe, the Nazis, the Ukrainians. Even in America, didn't they have white muggers?

Marlene turned again, once, twice. They were on a street with big wooden houses, porches, hedges, trees. You could pick it up and set it down in White Plains, not the newest part, the older part, and nobody would notice.

Marlene pointed to a house across the street, yellow with black shutters. "That's where Hitler grew up."

"Very nice. All right, not Hitler. You don't understand what I mean." God had moved her body next to Teddy's. He had moved Teddy, like a puppet, next to her. "Never mind Hitler. But remember the mugger. Central Park South."

"Teddy's not a mugger."

Fogel smiled at her ingratiatingly. Such is fatherhood in America: Parents must ingratiate themselves with their children. "I don't think personally he's a mugger."

"You're the mugger." Marlene pulled away from the curb, coming dangerously close to a big red convertible that was driving up the street toward her. "You're the mugger. You're mugging me."

"And you?" On the sidewalk a black boy was walking by with a heavy green book bag over his shoulder. "What do I have if I don't have my children?"

"Just don't be prejudiced. You don't want to be prejudiced." Marlene was driving too fast. She turned corners too fast. At intersections where signs said STOP, she barely touched the brakes. "Now I'm going to take you to the art museum. They have an eighteenth-century French room. When I saw it I said, 'My father would like this.' That's what I told Teddy, the exact words, 'My father would like this. My father is an eighteenth-century man.' "

"In the camps, I used to think of Versailles. What is the subject of Teddy's dissertation?"

"You told me about Versailles before. I told you about Teddy before. The image of blacks on TV."

Fogel's head hurt. Would his voice tremble when he talked? Would Marlene trick him and drive him to Harvard? Or to Brandeis again? But no, Marlene was pulling over to the curb. She pointed to a long low building made of marble, white and handsome, in classical style. "There it is, the museum." She turned the motor off.

Fogel opened his door and started to get out.

"Wait a minute!" Marlene suddenly smiled, happy and excited. She grasped Fogel's hand and pressed it against her stomach. "Here!" she said. "Feel!"

Fogel drew his hand away. "You felt? I didn't feel. What's to feel?"

Marlene started to take the car keys out of the ignition. Fogel reached over to grab her hand. "Here." Fogel pressed her hand against his forehead. "Here!" he said. "Here! Now you feel."

XIII

S teven, listen!'' Lillian had telephoned Los Angeles. "You
  know what happened? Yesterday he's lying down with
  his headache. I bring him a damp washcloth to put on
his forehead. I start putting it on for him and he grabs it
and throws it at me."

"He's had a hard life."

"And the same day he forgot Marlene is pregnant."

"People get older."

"Steven, I'm worried." Lillian covered the telephone
mouthpiece with her hand. She stood up and walked across
the kitchen to the dining-room door to make sure Fogel was
nowhere nearby where he could hear. "He keeps saying sick.
Headaches. Forgetting. Do you think the doctor made a mistake?"

"Go back for another examination." Steven walked over
to the window to see if Elissa's car had turned into the
driveway under the lemon trees.

"I'm afraid." Lillian crossed her fingers. "I have forebodings." She paused, emphasizing the drama of the words.
"Black forebodings."

In Los Angeles the lemon trees are green, in White Plains the forebodings are black, but in Boston there's only white to be seen.

Freak weather; an April snowstorm. Snow covered Commonwealth Avenue and glistened on the trolley tracks that run along the island at its center. Teddy's car, parked facing west heading out toward the Jewish suburbs, was buried under snow. The windshield was invisible, the tires almost completely white-walled.

"I'd better start shoveling out there." Heavy snowflakes were still falling. "Do you know what snow is?" Teddy hit the windowsill with his fist. "New England shit."

"Don't you think we should wait until morning so the snow stops? My water only broke ten minutes ago." Marlene rested her hand on her belly. She was silent for a moment. "We've got some leeway. There's no action in there now."

"It's already eleven-thirty. There's no way we're going to be able to put hands on a taxi tonight."

"We could call the cops and say it's an emergency."

"Then I'd have to hide in the closet." Teddy jumped away from the window and swung into a cakewalk step. He jazzed across the room and burrowed into the coat closet. "Nobody here but us niggers. I de cleanin' man. Dey jes' put me in here wid de mop an' de bucket af' I finish my wuk."

Marlene's suitcase was ready, her paperback baby books neatly packed. The date: April 11.

"Let's not call my mother now. Let's wait till I'm in the hospital. Nothing might happen till afternoon."

"I'm worried about leaving you if I go down to shovel."

"I'll sit in the window. You can see me."

"You better get your coat on though." Down below in the street a snowplow was now visible, laboring fiercely

155

through the whiteness. Teddy reached for his jacket and hurried out of the apartment, carrying the jacket in one hand and Marlene's suitcase in the other.

At the Beth Israel Hospital, the admitting-room clerk smiled briefly. "You're lucky to get here. You could have been killed." Then she became stern. "What's your Blue Cross-Blue Shield number?"

In preparation for this day, Teddy had learned the number by heart. Even before the clerk finished asking, he began reciting it to her.

"What's the hurry?" The clerk, a pale woman, made Teddy repeat the number. Six six six. Seven nine seven four. Very slowly, she wrote it down. Teddy nudged Marlene. Here it is, subtle but unmistakable—the baby's first experience with American racism.

"Private room or semi-private room?"

"Semi," Teddy said.

"Do you want a television set?"

"Yes."

"How about a telephone?"

"Yes."

"Kosher menu?" Again the clerk smiled.

"Certainly." Marlene nudged Teddy's back. "That's why I chose a Jewish hospital," she said.

Upstairs in the receiving room, nurses stared at Teddy indignantly. Two of them not only were dressed in white, they had white hair. "Have you called Dr. Bintz?" one asked.

"He said to wait even though my water broke. But then I started to feel something, so we came."

"I see." The nurse's eyes flickered. "Don't worry if Dr. Bintz doesn't get here in this snow. Anybody can deliver a baby."

156

Teddy began massaging Marlene's hand. On a night like this Bintz would be crazy to come out, even for a white man.

It was a blizzard. Four inches, five inches, Marlene was dilating. Outside the Beth Israel Hospital, snow covered Brookline Avenue. Behind the hospital, there was snow on Boston Latin School, the school of Benjamin Franklin, the school of John Quincy Adams, the school of Revere Garrison Jessep. Outside now, nothing but snow was visible, a snow-blitz: snowflakes, snow-whorls, treasuries of snow, snow-clutches, snow-caps, snow-down, Hansel-and-Gretel snow; six inches, seven inches, over the attics of Hyde Park; over the glass skylight of the Boston Aquarium where the weird, winter fishes swim, snow dimmed; a high Afro growing over Boston, an Afro turned white from fright.

Male baby Jessep: a monster. Terribly deformed, the arms twisted and limp, the head puffed with fluid, the eyes blank. Go describe it. It can't be done. Lips don't open to say words. Just the thought makes the mouth turn dry.

"I want to see," Teddy howled.

"No, you don't." A resident gripped Teddy's shoulder. Bintz had never made it. "Honest. Take my word for it. You don't want to see."

The new Teddy. The new Afro-Judeo-American.

"It won't live more than a day or two." One of the elderly nurses was swabbing Marlene's incision.

"My father killed it." Cold tears, like melting snow, ran down Marlene's cheeks.

Teddy walked past the observation room. The other babies lying there were all white—actually all red. One of them was being washed by a nurse. It had been born normal, but its narrow limbs looked like those of a concentration camp inmate.

In White Plains, Lillian walked into the living room where

a blue-and-white china bowl rested on the mantelpiece. "Perfect for sugar," she had said more than once. "Too bad there's no creamer to match it." Whenever she'd used it, Fogel always carefully restored it to its place, pushing it gently away from the edge of the mantel. "Meissen china! Fragile! Be careful. Valuable! This piece Lessing himself might have used." And the next day he'd check to make sure it hadn't been moved closer to the edge where dusting could knock it over, shattering the heritage of European civilization.

Cautiously, Lillian lifted the bowl off the mantelpiece and carried it into the kitchen where she set it on the countertop and began filling it with kosher salt, poured out of a big red-and-yellow box. Once the bowl was filled, she went to the dining-room cupboard where she kept her gift-wrapping material; she began raking through a drawer until she found a spool of red ribbon. She bit off a length and carried it into the kitchen too. From the knife rack on the kitchen wall, she took the sharpest knife. She set it on the kitchen counter next to the salt bowl and the ribbon. Then she reached up to get a jar of honey off the not-used-very-often shelf, and put a spoonful of honey into her mouth. With the sweet taste still in her mouth, she carried the salt bowl, the knife and the ribbon upstairs to the room where her daughter had slept before she'd been married; and she began to set them in position on the bed. The red ribbon for good luck went on top of Marlene's pillow. The bowl of salt went halfway down, at the place where the baby would come out. The knife for cutting pain went at the bottom, beneath Marlene's feet. "There!" Lillian said. "There!" In her heart she'd always known that the child would be born on the anniversary of Franklin Delano Roosevelt's death. Franklin Delano Roosevelt, the friend of the Negro and the Jew.

In Manhattan, Fogel sat in his office at NYU, beside his graduate student Levy, guiding Levy through some of the intricacies in the work of Pierre Bayle, especially Bayle's concept of Pyrrhonist skepticism, so influential in eighteenth-century thought. In the midst of Fogel's discussion of Pyrrhonism, the office telephone rang. Quickly, Fogel picked it up. Perhaps he had become a grandfather. Perhaps a new Fogel had been born, a replacement, even if dark. Indeed, it was Lillian on the telephone, but she had no baby news yet. Instead, she had a confession: "I just did something very silly."

"What did you do silly?" Fogel shrugged at Levy and thumped the page of Bayle's *Dictionnaire* (Abridged Version) which lay open on the desk. The message to Levy was clear: You read, while I talk on the telephone. Today, uncharacteristically, Levy was wearing a necktie and jacket, dressed as students should be dressed, as students formerly dressed, as perhaps Fogel's grandchild might someday dress. Certainly fashions change.

"It was silly, but I couldn't help it," Lillian explained. "A dish of salt is very important, my grandmother used to say." Lillian giggled. "I'm sure today is the day. That's why I did it. Superstitious, but what do I care?"

"Hell, hell," Fogel whispered into the telephone. Levy looked up at him, but Fogel again tapped the Bayle-page. Quickly, Levy looked down again and ran his finger from left to right along the page, as if he were following an especially difficult argument.

"What do you mean hell?" Lillian said. "Why hell? With a baby, you shouldn't say hell."

"Hell! Hell! This is what my grandfather used to say whenever he heard about superstition. Hell! Hell!"

Lillian's voice softened. "And now you're going to be a grandfather yourself."

"I am becoming a grandfather," Fogel said as he hung up the telephone.

Levy reached over to shake Fogel's hand. "Mazel tov!" he shouted. "Mazel tov! A boy or a girl?"

"Not yet. Not born yet." Fogel took his hand away. This was the hand his own grandfather had held. So life progresses! So the generations march forward! "Bayle," he said. "Bayle, in his discussion of Pyrrhonism, continues this important train of argument."

Levy looked down at the page conscientiously. "Did you yourself have a grandfather?" Fogel whispered.

Without student-shyness, Levy answered at once. "Sure. I had two of them." Levy leaned back in his chair, tilting it. "My mother's father I didn't know well. He was usually too busy for me. A doctor." A sadness-look darkened Levy's face. In future years, when thinking of his grandfather Fogel, such a sadness-look might appear on the face of Marlene's son, a face already darkened with Jew-sadness plus Negro-sadness, plus the sadness of grandfather-persecution, plus natural skin color. Levy smiled. "I didn't want to spend much time with him anyway because he always smelled of cigars."

But Levy also had good grandfather-memories, derived from his father's father, a clothing salesman who took him to see Yankee games, Mets games, Jets games, Ranger games. Fogel too had pleasant grandfather-memories of his father's father—not an enlightened man but a storekeeper, a grandfather who allowed Fogel to pick among the apples for rottens, a grandfather who held onto Fogel's hand whenever they took their Sabbath walk together. Alas, Marlene's son would have no Fogel grandfather-memories. Why? Because God had determined to destroy Fogel with headaches. "My grandfather?" Marlene's son would say. "You ask about my grandfather, the white one, the one who died of headaches. I never knew that grandfather."

Levy made a throat sound. Thinking about Marlene's baby—perhaps a girl, as pretty as Marlene but with darker skin color—Fogel had been silent too long. He tapped the page they had been studying. "Enough grandfather," he said. Tapping, thinking, tapping. Headache was tapping inside his temple. "Again Bayle."

"Ho, Grandmother!" Fogel called out as he walked through the kitchen door returning from school. There was no response. "Ho, Grandmother!" he shouted again. "Grandfather has come home." There was still no answer. "Ho, Grandmother!" he called again. Perhaps Lillian couldn't hear him.

Suddenly Lillian walked into the kitchen. She moved slowly. Her hair was ragged, her cheeks wet! Bad news! Fogel put out his arms. He reached over to embrace her. What was her reaction? She slapped his face. "You!" Again she slapped. "You call Steven and tell him. I can't tell him. All twisted! No nose! Hydrocephalic! I can't say the word. Hydrocephalic!"

Written in Magic Marker above the kitchen telephone were twenty numbers: Ten were Marlene's, ten Steven's. Fogel dialed. When Steven answered the telephone, was Fogel actually crying? Or was he chuckling? "Ya-haah! Ya-haah!" That was the sound he was making. Which was it, laughing or crying? It was hard for Steven to tell. "Bad. Bad news." Fogel was weeping. "I always knew bad."

"What are you saying?" Steven was buttoning the last button on his vest, getting ready to go out to the bars, a solo fling. What kind of a brother would go gallivanting around Los Angeles while his sister lay mourning on a hospital bed in Boston? "Is Marlene all right?"

161

No, Marlene is not all right.

"It's for the best," the hospital rabbi intoned. "Usually it's for the best."

Stroking Marlene's hair, Teddy nodded in agreement.

Marlene was crying again. "It's not for the best. I don't think it's for the best."

Teddy nodded in agreement. He was crying too.

"Is this what they mean when they say intermarriage is hardest on the children?" Teddy asked his mother. He had given in to her pleading and driven to Hyde Park for dinner. The wrought-iron flowers on one of her fancy kitchen chairs were pressing uncomfortably into his back. "They're wrong! It's harder on the parents."

Teddy was eating. His mother wasn't. His father hadn't put more than a spoonful of food into his mouth for two days. Only coffee. "And on the grandparents," Elora said. "Don't forget about the grandparents."

Grandfather Fogel! As it is written: Where are thy gods that thou hast made thee? Let them arise if they can save thee in the time of thy trouble.

Grandfather Fogel! As it is written: They have dealt treacherously against the Lord, for they have begotten strange children.

Grandmother Jessep, at the hospital, put her arms around Marlene and hugged her. She pressed her lips against Marlene's hair. "When you're pregnant again and get your real baby," she said, "then you'll know that's the baby you're really supposed to have."

Weakly, Marlene hugged back. Maybe these words were true. Maybe the next baby Marlene had would be the baby she was supposed to have. But meanwhile this baby was surviving.

Two days, four days. They didn't know what to do with it

162

at the hospital. Blue Cross pays, eighty percent, but only up to a certain point; after a while that point is reached. Could Marlene and Teddy bear putting the baby into an institution? Could they possibly take it home? There was a cradle waiting for it on Commonwealth Avenue, white wickerwork, a perfect match for the sofa. "Eventually," Marlene had said when she purchased it, "we'll be able to keep plants in it."

But no. Now, even the monster-baby couldn't be kept in it. Just before noon, day six, the hospital rabbi telephoned. The baby was dead. "It's customary to have a real funeral," the rabbi explained. "No matter who the Jew is, he has the benefit of a real funeral."

"It's not a customary Jew." Teddy twisted the telephone cord around and around. "We should just cremate it and scatter the ashes."

"No cremation." After three days without sobbing, Marlene broke down and cried again, pressing one of the red sofa pillows against her face. "There's already been too much cremation in this family. No more cremations. No."

Teddy hugged Marlene. "There'll be an honorable burial," he said. Marlene stopped crying.

On short notice, a burial plot is always available. Marlene telephoned her mother. "I'm sorry, but Daddy's going to have to drive up here again. Sharon Memorial Park. A beautiful place. They don't even have gravestones. Just bronze plaques."

"What are you going to put on the plaque?"

"I thought we'd name the baby Bryan Garrison Jessep after Daddy's grandmother, Bryna. Then, if the next one's a girl, we can name her Bryna."

"Not after my family!" Daddy was on the extension. "Not after my family, a monstrosity."

163

"You," Lillian shouted. "You're the monstrosity! You, not the baby!"

"You have to say Kaddish, Daddy." Marlene sounded mild and daughterly. "Teddy can't say it."

"Of course not." Lillian was crying.

"This I cannot do. I am a man of Enlightenment. I will not praise God. Not because of this, this child. Even for my own mother and father I have never said Kaddish."

LILLIAN COVERED every mirror in the house with the real-estate section of the Sunday *Times,* securing the newspaper pages with masking tape.

Now Fogel was a man in mourning. But if headaches had never kept him from going into the city to teach his class, to meet with his graduate student, to attend the weekly session of his therapeutic group, could such mourning do so? "Drive me," Fogel commanded his wife the next morning. "My train."

Wearing slippers instead of shoes as a sign that she was in mourning, Lillian drove to the station. "Even taking a shower didn't help my headache," Fogel informed her. "I think it's worse in the morning."

"I don't give a damn about your headaches anymore!" As Fogel got out of the car at the station, Lillian refused to lean over and kiss him good-bye. "You think other people don't have headaches too? I told you before. You're my headache. Hear that, Mr. Headache!" Lillian pressed down on the car horn. "Hear that! As soon as we come back from Boston, I'm taking you back to the doctor at Mount Sinai. You're acting so mental I think it must be physical."

"I will not say these prayers." Fogel sat in Dr. Wax's

office explaining the crisis in his life. He turned to Terry on his left, to Schwartz on his right. "I do not say prayers."

"But you made us say prayers." Now Terry was speaking directly to Fogel, a good sign. Therefore she no longer regretted the loft visit. "You made us go to the synagogue with you."

"What are you talking about?" Speaking directly, but rambling, Terry was talking oddly. Terry was a rambler, it must be admitted, an oddball. Now she was squinting her eyes.

"When we went to the synagogue."

Again Fogel inquired, "What are you talking about?"

Dr. Wax folded his hands like a Buddha-statue and stared, inspecting Fogel. Macy started to giggle. Then, after a look from Dr. Wax, he stopped. But Schwartz winked at Dr. Wax. "Professor Fogel is turning crazy," Schwartz said.

Fogel patted Terry's thigh. "For you I would pray." Let them giggle, let them laugh. Meanwhile Fogel had enjoyed. He kept his hand on Terry's thigh and squeezed. "For you. For the baby we could have together I would say a prayer. Not for this baby."

"We ain't having no baby together!" Terry pushed Fogel's hand away. "Not me."

Grabbing her hand, Fogel placed it on his own thigh. Though she tried to wriggle away, he held it tight. "Before, in the loft, you enjoyed it." Schwartz was gaping at him, ready to intervene. "Before you liked it. This I could tell."

Terry blushed. She stopped trying to twist her hand free. Dr. Wax was silent. Now, Charlotte of the subway panics was giggling. Schwartz was staring, standing up, standing over Fogel, leaning over him. He was shouting. "You mean you fucked her?"

165

"Sit down, Gerald," Dr. Wax commanded.

But Schwartz refused to sit down. "You fucked her?" he shouted again. Now suddenly Macy was standing up too, his face puffed with rage. He was leaning over Terry's chair. "You let that bastard and you won't let me."

"Sit down, Macy," Charlotte whispered.

Macy sat down. But Schwartz was still standing over Fogel threateningly. "I didn't *fuck* with him." Tears began to squeeze out of the corners of Terry's eyes. Her voice was shaking. "I didn't."

"What did you do?" Fogel's own voice was steady because Fogel was a steady man, a man of iron, a sophisticate among lunatics. "I don't forget the time together. What did you do? Never mind these people. To me say it."

"Just oral sex!" Terry shook her head as if she were trying to clear her memory. Or maybe dry her hair. Or maybe get a bad taste out of her mouth. "Big deal. Not so great either."

"You gave him a blow job?" This seemed to make Schwartz even angrier. This was how the Germans were angry: Fogel should not have the right to enjoy. The warmth of Schwartz's breath was disgusting. Dr. Wax jerked his head toward Charlotte. Charlotte understood his message. Quietly she got up, went over to Schwartz and, taking him by the arm, gently eased him back into his seat.

"Now," Dr. Wax said, "now, that episode's over."

"No, let her have my child, a child, a Jewish child. No, this is not an episode. No, it is not over. No, another child." Was Fogel shouting? Who cares? Did shouting make his head feel better? No.

"Shh!" Charlotte stood over Fogel, stroking his shoulder. "Shh!"

"Never mind shh!" Fogel brushed her away. "You shh!"

166

He leaned forward and roughly pushed her on the arm. "Away! You, away!" Charlotte's face seemed to crumple. She retreated back to her chair. Fogel turned to Dr. Wax. "Tell me, Dr. Wax. Tell me, this pain is in my mind, not in my head."

"That's what I've always said." But now Dr. Wax was ignoring Fogel. Fogel's money was being wasted. Dr. Wax was attending to Charlotte. "It's all right, Charlotte. Don't worry. You'll be all right. You'll be OK. He didn't hurt you, Charlotte. You're not hurt." Now Charlotte was stroking her own shoulder. Macy held onto her hand.

Fogel made a noise like an animal. "Gghh! In my head, not in my mind! This is what you think? It is in my head!"

With a small voice, Terry ventured a suggestion. "Maybe it's a tumor. Tumors can give headaches."

Dr. Wax shook his head philosophically. "Fortunately, they've found out it's not a tumor."

"Fortunately, unfortunately." Fogel stood up and shook his fist at Dr. Wax. "I have theories also, not only psychiatrists have theories, also professors have theories. I have my own theory. You!" Fogel pointed at Dr. Wax. "You! Do you wish to hear my theory?"

"Of course." Dr. Wax smiled.

"This is what I believe. This!" Fogel was shouting. How soundproof could Dr. Wax's office be? Fogel was yelling. "This is what I believe. They made a mistake at Mount Sinai."

"Sit down, Chaim," Dr. Wax ordered.

Certainly Fogel would not sit down.

"If it makes you feel any better," Dr. Wax's voice was intended to be soothing, "go back to the doctor and get it checked again."

Fogel moved toward the door, stumbling. His leg was shaking again. "I leave. I go. No more psychotherapy. No

167

more God-praying. No more magic. No more nothing. I go. Finished. You are Dr. Wax. Correct! You are all wacks. Wackos. Wackies." He opened the door and pointed a finger at Schwartz. "Lady!" Now he was pointing at Terry. "You too. A wacko. Furthermore a slut."

"Guten Tag!" Bowing as if he were Lessing leaving the presence of the Duke of Brunswick, Fogel stood in the doorway and then, quietly, moved back a step and shut the door. Through the closed door, he could hear Schwartz shouting, "Fuck you!" after him. This proved what he had all along suspected: Dr. Wax's office was not soundproof. Fogel pressed his ear against the door crack, but now all he could hear was a mumbling, a murmuring, a roaring, a sound like the sound all the alphabets in the world make at the moment when they are mingled together.

XIV

A gain I have created darkness. It is beginning to cover Grandfather Fogel. Outside his bedroom window, White Plains is becoming Black Plains. Within the bedroom where he lies facedown on the bed, listening on the telephone extension while Lillian is talking, pouring her heart out to her aunt Sarah-Who-Never-Shuts-Up, darkness has transformed the beautiful blue bedroom rug: Now it is gray. In hope of alleviating his head pain, Grandfather Fogel has been lying on the bed since he arrived home from his final psychotherapy visit. But bed rest isn't helping.

Darkness has already covered Grandfather Fogel's grandson, the monster-baby, whose corpse lies in an unlighted room beneath the cherrywood pews of a Jewish funeral parlor in Brookline, Massachusetts. In Lvov, in Stoianov, I have created light. In the house in Stoianov where Fogel's own Grandfather Fogel once lived, rising each morning to thank Me for making him a Jew and wearing, as I have commanded, My Great Name beside his heart and on his brow, a Ukrainian schoolteacher now is rising. Wake-up music surges out of his radio. In the morning light his wife cooks sausage-bits for his breakfast. In Lvov, in the apartment where Fogel lived as a child—not the first apartment but the apartment overlooking the trolley tracks—sausage is also being cooked. When Jews lived in these rooms, pork-smells never ascended within their walls. Bergen-Belsen is still in darkness. Auschwitz is still in darkness. There I have not yet created light.

"I was too proud," Lillian said. "I was too pleased. I was a pig. That's why it happened. It's my punishment." For an hour she had been talking on the telephone to Sarah-Who-Never-Shuts-Up.

"A demon, a demon!" Sarah answered. "An evil eye. Witchwork. Not because Marlene married with a colored man. Not because she married with a Gentile. He was wearing a yarmulke, didn't I see! A beautiful wedding. God doesn't think that way. God forbid! It's not your fault, it's not Marlene's fault, somebody has it in for her, maybe for you, maybe for the husband, who knows, colored people, the in-laws, who can tell, they seemed like nice people, I shouldn't be saying, Jews also, maybe one of your neighbors, who knows?" Sarah paused, but only for a moment. Then she started talking again. "Listen, Lillian. God helps. You make sure the little one is circumcised before they put him into the ground. Marlene is Jewish, right? She didn't make a conversion to Christian, right?"

"Maybe Teddy will convert." Lillian's grip tightened on the receiver. "He's been thinking about it."

"Jewish, a Jewish baby, a Jewish boy. There's no question about it. So this is what you need: circumcised, wine-drinking, blessings, the prayers, done right, the whole works. The poor little boy, did he ever stand a chance? And now if no circumcision, he doesn't pass through the gate."

"But he's already dead."

"It doesn't matter. To God, do you think that makes any difference? He was a Jew, that means he should have a circumcision."

Fogel pressed down the telephone receiver. He sat up and wiped the corner of his eye with the edge of the pillowcase. Not a tear, merely headache-juice. Then, quickly, he picked up the telephone again. Finally, Lillian had hung up. Using his eye-wiping finger, he started turning the telephone dial: ten numbers, information.

He made his inquiry politely. But the operator—obviously a novice, obviously not suited for work requiring diplomacy—challenged him. "Isn't that spelled UP not EP?" she asked, even though her job was to answer inquiries not to make them. "EP," Fogel responded with dignity. Only then did the operator fulfill her proper function: She whipped a chain of numbers at Fogel in a metal voice. Head pains, death camps, monster-babies—can these affect a scholar's carefully cultivated powers of concentration? Certainly not!

Fogel memorized Marlene's number and dialed it. Once, many months before, he had refused to learn this number. "I have had enough of black numbers," he had said when Lillian reproached him for not learning it. Now he knew it. Ten more numbers were stored away in the cells of his brain.

"Go out. Buy. Spend," Fogel whispered as soon as Marlene answered the telephone. "Nice clothes for this baby. Not a gravesheet. Go, purchase, carry to the funeral man. Tell him this is what your father wants."

Why was Marlene remaining silent? Why saying nothing? Should a father's call be greeted this way, like a call from a stock-market-seller? Does not Chaim Fogel have the right to be concerned about his own grandson, the child of his daughter, a daughter who proves to be a loyal Jew and not, as he had once feared, a betrayer of the generations? No words had come out of Marlene's mouth yet, nothing but a "Hello," merely a formality. A daughter in mourning, true, but also a grandfather in mourning. Is not a grandfather entitled to mourn too? But then slowly, quietly, Marlene's words came twisting along the telephone wire: "I didn't know you cared."

"Certainly I care. This is why I am calling in the midst of my travel preparations. I insist: nice clothes. Too many Jews into graves without nice clothes—shot, burned, murdered, killed. Now nice, maybe a velvet suit, a pretty collar. Don't worry money. I pay. Furthermore, Marlene—" Suddenly Fogel's voice began to scrape. "Furthermore, you make sure this: Before you bury, circumcise! A Jewish mother, a Jewish child. The father doesn't matter. Only the mother. A Jewish baby, therefore circumcise!"

Fogel let his head fall back against the pillow. He set the telephone on his chest: Princess model, light as a feather. Now he could rest, now he could be comfortable, lying relaxed, even if in what his guru book called the corpse position. Certainly not a completely Gentile baby! Certainly a baby who would have been sent off to die with other Jews. Are there not black Jews in Ethiopia, also persecuted? Why not in Boston too, but not persecuted—not yet. "Not circumcised in order to go through the gate," Fogel said. He began laughing. Not funny, a dead child. Nevertheless, lying on the bed, in the midst of a consolation call, at this idea, Fogel laughed. Amusing: the gate. "The gate, heaven, superstition, religion, this is what your mother believes. Why? From listening to her crazy aunt, crazy Sarah, that's why.

"Crazy! Foolish, all foolish—God, heaven, praying, gates. This is not why to circumcise." Fogel stopped laughing. No longer was it a time for laughing. Now it was a time to be serious, to explain, to instruct the next generation—a father's sacred duty, also a professor's. "Do you know why to circumcise? Do you know?"

From Marlene no answer came.

"I will tell you why. Here is why. Because there is only one thing an enlightened man can believe. What thing is that? I tell you what thing. History, that is what thing. Isn't this correct?"

Again no answer came. "History. Isn't this correct? Don't you agree? Right?"

"Right," Marlene whispered.

"History equals circumcision. Incontrovertible! Superstitious, certainly, nevertheless historical. With headaches, without headaches, God nothing, forget God, ditto religion; but do not forget history. History, this I always believed. So also Voltaire. Therefore, circumcise. Also for the other babies, the cousins. These babies you never knew. Even I never knew. Why? Because these babies never were born."

"Daddy, is Mommy there?"

"She is here." So what if no longer talking to Daddy. Need Marlene know this? "Preparing to leave. I am ready to leave. Going, gone. Marlene?"

Marlene grunted.

"Are you planning again to have a baby? This baby didn't, it didn't, discourage?"

"Let's bury this one first."

"Of course, bury. First circumcise, then bury." Fogel paused: a moment of silence. The moment ended. "I will give you a pep-talk. Pep-talk is how Jews survive." In the camps, did not Fogel give himself pep-talk while other Jews, not survivors, prayed? Although—truth is truth—certain praying Jews also survived. Is not praying itself a species of pep-talk? No matter! "Here is my pep-talk: No discouragement! Courage equals babies. History proves this." Fogel shifted the telephone from his chest onto the bed and sat up

173

again. "History makes Jews. Therefore circumcise. They think: Good-bye Jews, PLO, Arabs, Nazis, Ukrainians, camps, ovens, etcetera, etcetera. But circumcised, not good-bye.

"Now I have given my message." Fogel rubbed his forehead with his fist. "So my grandfather would speak, a dead man from the grave, not from the grave, actually from the air. So I speak, also a grandfather, still living, no grave yet. I hear your mother." Indeed, downstairs Lillian was shuffling from one room to another. "So, good-bye." Without waiting for a good-bye from Marlene—Did she chat? Did she converse as a daughter should? At his grave she would say good-bye—Fogel hung up.

"What gate is he talking about?" Teddy was sitting on the wicker sofa holding Marlene's hand. "Pearly? That it? Pearly? He's out of his mind, your daddy. How can they circumcise a corpse? They keep calling us Africans savages. It's them that's savages." Teddy let go of Marlene's hand. "I thought all this kosher business was crazy enough—milk dishes for the milk foods, meat dishes for the meat foods. A whole religion built around pots and pans. But this is even crazier. Putting a knife into a baby's corpse like that! Who's going to do that? Not on my kid, they don't."

Marlene reached for Teddy's hand again. "If that's what my father wants, we have to investigate it."

Investigation:

Over the telephone, the hospital rabbi made his pronouncement. "No! Absolutely not! Absolutely unnecessary! Circumcising that baby now isn't Judaism! It's superstition!" The rabbi forced gentleness into his voice: He was speaking to a bereaved mother. "Merely a superstition," he said. "They may have done things like that in Europe, though I've never heard of it. There were a lot of strange ideas circulating around in Europe. Your father must have picked

174

some of them up. But no responsible Jewish authority"—again sternness weighted the rabbi's voice—"would consider doing such a thing. If the baby had lived for eight days, it would have been circumcised. But he lived only six days."

"Are you sure?" Marlene listened for a minute. Then she said, "Thank you for your help." Teddy took the telephone receiver out of her hand and put his arms around her. "Let's just tell your father we did it and forget about it. He'll never know."

Marlene moved her shoulders so that Teddy's arms had to drop away. "I won't lie to him." She picked up the telephone and dialed White Plains.

Fogel made his pronouncement. "Never mind rabbis, what they say. Foolishness! On the eighth day, kosher; on the seventh day, superstitious. Don't worry. Foolish! You go to bed. Tomorrow, we find a way. Don't worry money. I give the money. Money buys. This I saw, even in the camps. Not, unfortunately, in the death camps—there no more money, nobody had—but in the work camps. Money buys life. Also through the gate. This for your mother, this for her auntie. Not for me. Me, I don't care. To me what is this gate? Nothing. I have learned this: Superstitions cannot help headaches. Nevertheless we will do. We will accomplish. You don't worry, you sleep, get back your health."

Elora, delivering a homemade apple pie and a beef stew, made her pronouncement. "Cut it, cut it. Poor little soul. If he's going to be a Jew, he's going to be a Jew. The aunt is right. She's a nice woman. I remember her at the wedding. Very nice. You listen to that lady, Teddy. Never mind what the rabbi says. He doesn't know anything about how Marlene feels."

At the funeral parlor the director, Mr. Tick, in a dark gray suit and a black-and-gray-striped necktie, made his pronouncement. "Out of the question! No." He touched Marlene's arm. "I know how you must feel. Terrible. Personally, I'd like to oblige you, but I have to do business in the Jewish community. If word went out that we were performing rituals according to strange superstitions rather than according to traditional Jewish law, I'd go bankrupt in a week."

"Even if it's a Jewish superstition?" Teddy asked.

"There are superstitions and there are superstitions." What Mr. Tick meant by this, neither Teddy nor Marlene knew.

"My father is insisting on it." Marlene waited, as if these words alone would clinch the argument. She held the next sentence back for a second. Then she delivered it. "He's a Holocaust survivor. Bergen-Belsen."

Tick's eyes screwed up, his nose wrinkled grotesquely, his lips twisted open, showing yellow teeth. He shook his head from side to side and made a "tt" sound. But he didn't say anything.

"If my wife can find a circumciser who will circumcise on your premises," Teddy said softly, "would you allow him access?"

Again Tick shook his head from side to side: No. He stared at Marlene who was clutching a rolled-up handkerchief and pressing it against her cheek. Then he whispered another pronouncement: "Yes." He blinked. "Try calling the Hebrew Rehabilitation Center in West Roxbury. Ask for Mr. Bitsky. He's a mohel."

Marlene turned to Teddy to explain. "A circumciser."

For the "mohel" Teddy needed no explanation. It was the words "Rehabilitation Center" that puzzled him.

"Why do they call it a rehabilitation center?" he asked as he walked into the building with Marlene after an hour of driving through rush-hour traffic. Five or six frail-looking inmates sat in the center's entrance hall, on modern over-stuffed chairs, watching hungrily for visitors. "These folks aren't ever going to be rehabilitated."

"I think they get more government money if they call it a rehabilitation center."

Bitsky was a fat, bald old man, stale-smelling and wearing a rumpled, itchy-looking gray sweater. "Why don't you go to an active mohel?" His eyes were bloodshot. "Why come to me?"

Marlene explained why.

The old man began buttoning up his sweater. "A real problem," he said. "A real problem."

"That's why we came to you, sir." Teddy tried to smile.

"You don't have to smile at me." Bitsky reached over and pinched Marlene's cheek. "So you are white, a pretty little Jewish girl. And you," he turned to Teddy, "are a pumpernickel. In Boston this matters." He clenched his fist, giving Teddy a thumbs-up sign, pointing to the ceiling and beyond. "But up there, so what!" Bitsky's hand opened. He began waving it back and forth in a wide arc, suddenly and surprisingly light and delicate. The waving gradually slowed down. The arc became tighter. The old man's stiff index finger was pointing at Marlene. "You are very sad." The index finger jabbed at the air in front of Marlene's face. "You don't know why God should do this to you. Now you have to stop worrying. God will give you another baby." Without pausing to take a breath, the old man suddenly started singing in an archaic synagogue voice—a slow, beating Hebrew song. One word in the song both Marlene and Teddy recognized, *chaim,* the word that means "life."

Sing, Jew! These words are My pleasure.

These are the words I hear when the plants and animals are singing to Me:

"Remember us for life, King Who Delights in Life. Inscribe us in the Book of Life, for Your sake, Living God!"

"Beautiful," Teddy said when Bitsky stopped singing. "What does it mean?"

The old man leaned forward and pinched Marlene's cheek a second time. Then he stroked it. "What it means is this: Cheer up! Do you want to hear another cheer-up?"

Marlene brushed her cheek. Seeing that, Bitsky folded his hands on his lap. "Yes," Marlene said, "I need cheering up."

The old man took his hands off his lap, held them up and rubbed them together. "See. Big. But careful. A mohel's hands." He put his hands back on his lap. "A careful cutter. Don't worry." He stretched his hand out again; this time it was Teddy he touched, on the arm. "For your next baby, I'll recommend someone else to perform for you. But with this baby"—he paused for a moment and then delicately continued—"I'm not too old."

Suddenly, he began singing Hebrew words again, rocking from side to side as he sang. "Merciful," he said in English when he had finished singing. "Merciful and compassionate. That's what this means. And as for the blood drops, it doesn't matter."

Marlene covered her face with her hands. "Are you sure you'll do it?"

"Don't worry. You drive me there and I'll perform. Then you drive me home."

"My father said to drink wine."

"After. You buy the wine. I make the blessing." The old man pointed at Teddy. "Only one glass for you, mister. You have to drive this lady home. Leave the bottle here."

178

"How do we pay you?" Teddy said.

The old man reached over to stroke Marlene's cheek, twisting his lips as if to say: Don't stop me, I don't care, I will play, I will touch, I will feel. "This is my price: Invite me to the next baby's circumcision."

"IT'S ALL DONE, wine, the whole works," Marlene said when Fogel picked up the kitchen telephone. Two suitcases containing funeral clothes had just been loaded into the car. Lillian was still in the upstairs bathroom, rubbing foundation cream into her cheeks, especially under the eyes where tears had affected her skin tone. But the more she rubbed, the more tears came.

"We just got back from the funeral parlor," Marlene said. "All done, blessings, everything. The mohel was named Mr. Bitsky." The name Bitsky proved that Marlene was telling the truth: It was a name nobody could invent.

"Good," Fogel said. "Good. What I ask you to do, you do. This is good, but is it really good? Is it foolishness? Is it barbarism? Why bother? Why circumcise a dead baby, a baby already deformed? To please your mother? To please her crazy aunt Sarah? To please crazy God? This I know: To make a circumcision work, you must see blood drops. Is it possible for a corpse to produce blood drops? Do you know? I have seen many corpses, still I don't know this."

Marlene wasn't answering. Had she stopped listening? Even her breathing couldn't be heard. Silence, as if she had quietly hung up the telephone in the middle of the conversation, while her father was still speaking. Nobody was listening. Nobody was there. Perhaps even Fogel himself was not there. Perhaps this time it was really true: Fogel was already dead.

No, it was not true. Dead men tell no tales. Fogel would tell a tale. Therefore, Fogel was alive. Perhaps this tale would comfort Marlene, perhaps console her, perhaps help her. "Marlene," Fogel said. "Marlene, let me tell you this." Not a fairy tale, such as he used to tell Marlene—the snow maiden, the apple girl. A true tale. "Marlene, let me tell you, once in Lvov I saw many dead babies, a pile. Maybe Ukrainian babies, maybe, but I don't think so. Certainly Jewish babies. Marlene." Marlene was not answering. "Marlene, are you listening to me? Some not just babies, some already children, but most of them babies, little. And Marlene—" There was still no response from Marlene, nothing but silence on the telephone wire, a vacuum, dead silence. "Marlene, all of these babies were dead just like your baby, not only dead, also dark. They were black. They were turned colored!"

The receiver clicked up and down as if the phone were broken, as if Marlene were trying to reach the operator— each click breaking the connection with Fogel and then reestablishing it, then breaking it, then reestablishing it: Click! Click! Click! until suddenly all Fogel could hear was a mechanical whine, worse than silence, worse than dead-phone noise, a sound invented by the telephone company to tell telephone users that all the connections had ended, all the impulses stopped. They were no longer in touch.

"Marlene!" Fogel cried when he heard the awful noise. "Marlene!" He moved the telephone receiver away from his head and held it in his hand. He shook the receiver up and down, three times, four times, again and again. He held the receiver in front of his face, immobile, with his head immobile too. He sat staring at it. "Marlene!" he called out. "Marlene! Marlene!" There was no answer. "Marlene! Am I already dead?"

180

XV

Exalted, compassionate God, grant perfect peace in Your sheltering Presence among the holy and pure who shine with the splendor of the firmament to the soul of our dear Bryan Garrison Jessep who has gone to his eternal home."

The cemetery is white with snow. Half of the mourners standing beside the grave-canopy are black. The corpse itself is half-black, though no one has actually seen it. Many Jesseps are there. One of Lillian's cousins has come all the way from New Jersey. From the splendor of the firmament, dead Fogels look down, particularly the late Bryna Fogel. But Steven hasn't come. All the way from California? In California he might be getting—on the phone with Lillian, he had laughed with excitement—"backing for a film. I think I can get it. Let me talk to Daddy."

"A Jewish film this time." This news Steven mumbled to his father, as if he were shy about making such a film. "Too late," Fogel mumbled back. "For me, too late. You want me to say hallelujah? I'll say it: Hallelujah." Should Steven have traveled from California to film this funeral? The Death of the Jews, Part 999. In black and white.

The rabbi is holding a thick red book in his hand. Usually when Fogel went to funerals, the rabbi held a little blue book, put out by the Funeral Directors' Association. But this is a special case, an unusual funeral, the death of an unusual Jew. For his own burial—how much longer? a week? a month?—they would use the regular book. "Despite the sick, despite the dead, despite the cries of pain, I rise to praise my Lord." These words would be recited over Fogel's corpse by a rabbi who had never known him. But what rabbi actually could know? What person in history could know?

"May his soul always be bound up in the bond of life." Fogel's soul is fleeing from his mouth, he can see its steamy exhalation in the cold. The rabbi is looking at him, Lillian is looking at him. Again, again, again: He is the one in the tiny coffin, it is he of whom the rabbi has sung, "Master of mercy, remember all his worthy deeds." The time at Bergen-Belsen when he had refrained from striking Moishke Fingernails, a Jew who enjoyed lifting the hands of exhausted prisoners and inspecting their nails to see if they'd live through the night. Or the time he had given a C−, not an F, to a black student—engineering—who was worried that otherwise he wouldn't be able to graduate. And this good deed as well: surviving. But it is finished.

Lillian is tugging at Fogel's coat sleeve. The rabbi is holding out a book. He's pointing to the page where the prayer for the dead is written, his finger runs across the English transliteration beneath the prayer just in case Fogel is unable to read Hebrew. "Recite," the rabbi whispers. "Yisgadal v'yisgadash."

"Magnified and sanctified," Marlene murmurs.

Fogel snorts, a sound which could be mistaken for a sob, but he accepts the book from the rabbi and holds it before his eyes in reading position. Gently, Marlene takes it out of his hands and turns it right side up. It is absolutely silent in

the graveyard. On the snowy ground, a black gravedigger
stands outside the little circle, leaning on his shovel. Tears
fall silently down the cheeks of Elora Jessep. There's a noise.
Teddy's father is breathing hoarsely. But again it is silent.
God is listening. Fogel begins to recite.

"One four eight nine," he calls out. "One four eight
nine."

"Kaddish," Lillian cries.

"Three." Fogel is holding the book properly, yet Marlene
is staring at him. The rabbi, even Teddy, stand with their
mouths open as if Fogel is crazy. "Three point one four one
five nine."

Teddy's parents looked puzzled. Is this the first Jewish
funeral they've ever been to? Marlene moves over to stand
beside her father. She points to the prayer in the book. Her
hand is on his arm.

"Eight six six four two seven." Fogel is chanting. His
voice is loud, not choked and swallowed like some mourners'
voices. "Eight six six four two seven."

Marlene takes the prayer book out of Fogel's hand. She
grabs Teddy's hand and pulls him beside her. She begins
praying in Hebrew. "Yisgadal." After she says the word, she
pauses and looks at Teddy. Teddy repeats it. "Yisgadal."
"V'yisgadash," Marlene says. This too Teddy repeats. Marlene: "Sh'mai rabah." Teddy: "Sh'mai rabah." White.
Black. White. Black. Jew. Gentile. Jew. Gentile. All nations
shall sing His praises. Teddy has his arm around Marlene,
practically touching her breast, he's holding her tight, tight;
this is a foretaste. What do you do after a funeral? First you
cry, then you try. You make life. For the young, yes. For the
old, no. Fogel puts his hands on his forehead. He is weeping.
His head. His head. Lillian puts her arms out, she folds her

arms around his head, he puts his head on her breast, his back is to the grave. "Yisborach," Marlene says. "Yisborach," Teddy says, pronouncing the *ch* beautifully. Now he has an impeccable Hebrew accent.

"Millions," Fogel whispers. "Millions."

"Numbers? What do you mean numbers?" Lillian and Fogel have stopped at a Howard Johnson's on the Massachusetts Turnpike for a snack. Why? "Because I'm starving, that's why. Because you have your headache and I'm the one doing the driving. Therefore, I decide where the car goes, that's why. Because I can't drive this distance after my grandson's funeral, my first grandchild, without eating. That's why!" Lillian was so angry that the car swerved dangerously.

"Careful! Careful! Careful!"

"Because you won't go to Teddy's mother's house. Because you make a face when Teddy's mother invites us. Because I have to make excuses, that's why." Indeed, when the invitation came—"Just some little cakes," Elora had said. "Just some food the neighbors brought in"—Fogel had clutched his forehead.

"He's not feeling well," Lillian had explained.

Now Lillian was having a bowl of New England clam chowder, a Howard Johnson's specialty. "The numbers. You were supposed to be saying Kaddish, you said numbers. Insane. Everything but the telephone number." Lillian put down her soup spoon and wiped her eyes with her napkin. "Everything but the Zip Code."

"What are you talking about?" Fogel was also having New England clam chowder. It was every bit as good as African peanut soup. "You're crazy. Marlene asks me to say Kaddish. I say Kaddish. Yisgadal. Yisgadash. She asks me, I say it. What do I care? What does it matter? Although"—Fogel winked at Lillian—"I have a theory. What do you think? This is it. God is the cause of anti-Semitism."

Lillian stared.

"This is the explanation. God is omnipotent, correct? This makes people feel powerless. Whose fault is it that there's a God? The Jews' fault, correct? Therefore, when people feel powerless, they attack the Jews. Is this an original theory?"

Now Lillian's eyes were as dry as stone. Her mouth was dry too. She pushed her bowl of soup away, unfinished. "To-morrow, first thing, you go to the doctor."

"Tomorrow first thing, no! Tomorrow, first thing, I fly on an airplane to Detroit. Why was I not chosen to be on the board of editors for the Lessing Society Yearbook? I go to confront the Wayne State University Press." Having finished his own soup, Fogel reached over to take Lillian's chowder bowl and set it down next to his own. "You aren't going to finish it," he said. "I'll eat it."

"Finish it." Lillian ripped open a sugar packet and poured a mound of sugar grains onto the table. She pressed her thumb into the sugar mound. Sugar grains spread across the yellow plastic. "You are a man without emotion."

Fogel splashed his spoon into Lillian's chowder bowl. He resumed eating.

Lillian picked up a cellophane-wrapped package of crackers which had come with the soup and held it in her hand for a moment. Then she shut her fist around it and crushed it. "I can't stand you. I can't stand you anymore," she whispered. Her teeth showed. Her lips were almost invisible. "You're so crazy. For almost a year now, crazy. Since you went to the psychiatrist. Even before. Crazy." She spoke so quietly that no one in the adjoining booths could hear.

Fogel rapped his spoon against a water glass. He called

loudly, "Waitress, waitress, where is my check?" With an energetic smile, the waitress hurried over to the table. While she was adding up the check, Fogel reached into his pocket for money. He crumpled a five-dollar bill and threw it on the table.

"You're supposed to pay at the cashier's booth," the waitress said in a too-clear voice. But Fogel stood and picked up his coat. Without putting it on, without waiting for change, he walked out. "My husband is becoming a lunatic," Lillian said to the waitress. The waitress winked at her.

"What are you talking about, numbers?" Fogel shouted when Lillian got into the car. "What do you mean?" He had taken over the driving. Pressing down on the accelerator angrily, he started the car and moved out quickly into the turnpike traffic, although an enormous Greyhound bus was approaching fast.

Lillian shouted back, she was louder than the bus's brakes, she was screeching: "Do you want to get me killed? Is that it? Take your tootsies, take your bunnies, I don't care, all you want, just don't drive so stupid." She began to cry. "You've gone crazy. I used to think, last year, this was the camps, the man has suffered, let him be, so he's a little eccentric, air baths, so bear with it. But I can't stand you anymore. I think you're getting demented. That's what I think." She ripped a paper towel off the roll Fogel kept in the front seat in case the windshield got steamed up. "Just leave me alone, will you! I'm the one who should go to a psychiatrist, not you. I need the help. You crazy isn't bad enough. You're driving me crazy, you're making me sick, all I put up with. 'No erratic behavior,' we said to the doctor at Mount Sinai. 'No erratic behavior.' " Lillian rubbed her eyes with the paper towel. "I don't want to jump to conclusions, I don't want conclusions. But it frightens me."

All through Connecticut she was crying, silently, ripping paper towels and rubbing her face with them. Finally, near New Haven, Fogel whispered, "Do you want me to stop? I can get for you. There's a box of tissues in the trunk."

"If I want tissues, I have tissues in my pocketbook."

"You are giving me a headache."

Choking laughter was Lillian's response.

"Laugh! Laugh!" Fogel tightened his grip on the steering wheel. "God is laughing too. The psychiatrist is laughing, also the gurus." He pressed his foot harder against the ac- celerator. The car lurched forward. "No more psychiatrist for me! No more acupuncture! No more biofeedback. No more synagogue, no more anything. Finished."

"Slower!" Lillian screamed.

Fogel lifted his foot off the accelerator. The speedometer needle sank back, wavered, rested at forty—too slow, under the legal speed. "Your concept is also my concept." Under the speed limit, over the speed limit, what difference could it make? "Certainly they made a mistake at Mount Sinai. Certainly they misinterpreted my brain. This I have always suspected." Fogel inhaled—a deep, highway-fume inhale. So what highway-fumes! So what death gas! "Never mind a trip to Detroit for me. Never mind Wayne State University Press. Tomorrow again I will visit the medical doctor."

The telephone was ringing as Fogel walked into the house. "You answer it," he said to Lillian. "Me, directly to bed."

It was Steven calling. "Teddy says Daddy should go for another checkup. I telephoned Marlene."

"Tomorrow we go. Tomorrow." Lillian put her hand on her forehead. Now she too had a headache. "Today he agrees: We go tomorrow. Tomorrow, who knows? Tomorrow maybe he'll throw something at me again."

Does Steven ask details? No. An artist is concerned with

187

too many details already: lighting, character, point-of-view, theme, particularly in this film, theme. Finally: total Jewish content. Some of the other films had Jewish elements. *Ghetto Wedding at the St. Moritz* did; even the Hare Krishna film had a little. But none of them had total Jewish content. This one: out-and-out Jewish.

Steven, hear My voice!

Like your father you declare: "Up to a point Jewish. . . . Maybe a little Jewish. . . . Maybe perhaps Jewish."

Foolish Jew! There is no "Perhaps Jewish." And there is no "Up to a point Jewish." There is no escaping My command.

Yin Yang Jerusalem. Chapter Twelve: Holocaust.

Get a book of matches, the kind that's given away when a pack of cigarettes is purchased. Open your copy of the Bible to Isaiah, chapter 45, verse 7. Read the verse aloud:

I form the light and create darkness: I make peace, and create evil: I the Lord do all these things.

Strike one of the matches. Stare into the flame. Do not let go of the match even though the flame is burning down fast. Your finger will feel hot. You may become worried about being burned. Nevertheless, allow the flame to singe your fingertip. Feel the pain, if only for an instant. The match is almost consumed. Quick! Blow the fire out! You are using the breath of life to blow out the flame. There are twenty matches in the matchbook. On the following page are twenty Bible verses, one for each match. Read each verse and then repeat the process with each match. It is better not to do all of this exercise in one day. Spread it out over weeks or even months, and then, if desired, repeat it with another matchbook.

"This one's crazy," Steven's Buddhist girlfriend had said. "I'll watch, but I won't play." Steven had used up two matchbooks. For the third matchbook, he invited someone else to play, a new girl, Rochelle, who worked at the Holocaust Foundation. Rochelle was an enthusiastic player, using up an entire matchbook of her own on Exodus 3:2, "Behold the bush burned with fire and the bush was not consumed."

"A completely Jewish film," Steven said to Lillian on the telephone. "I think I'm going to shoot it in New Jersey. A flat landscape. I don't want to use mountains."

Upstairs in the bedroom, above the telephone conversation, Fogel was sitting buttoning his pajamas, catching his breath. The television was on: world news, again Israel. Suddenly Fogel began to bend in his chair, as if he were folding. "God!" he screamed. "God! God!" His head was down on his hands, his hands were on his lap. He started to gag, he vomited onto Lillian's blue-flowered bedroom chair, onto Lillian's carpeting. An animal, a wild thing, a gouger, twisting and biting.

Not in the camps—not the pisslicking, not the hungry, not the afraid, not the smell of dying bodies, not the guards' smiling—nothing like this. Fogel stumbled down onto the floor, his head touched carpet, tears came out of his eyes, he scrambled over to the bed, he grabbed a pillow and pressed it against his face. Still, gouging. Inside his head, a commercial: a petroleum-voiced man making promises. Aspirin. Aspirin. Again he screamed.

"What? What?" Lillian ran into the room. "What, Chaim? What?" She grabbed his shoulders and began to shake him. "What?"

He was sitting on the bed, the pillow smothering his head. "Off." He waved at the television set.

Lillian ran over to shut it. Another sound—whistling, a growl, as if out of a dog gullet.

Lillian's arm went around Fogel. He shook her away. His

189

fist hit her breast. His fist beat at the mattress, at her shoulder, at her shoulder, at his chest, his stomach, her arm, her back, the pillow, his head. "Chaim!" She was roaring. "What?"

"A knife! A knife!" He rocked his head from side to side. There were sobbing sounds in his head.

"Now!" Lillian ran over to the closet and got out a pair of his shoes. She knelt down in front of him and took off his slippers. She squeezed his feet into the shoes. "Now." She ran out of the room and returned in a minute. She put a coat on Fogel. Holding his arm, she guided him downstairs. "Wait." It was raining. She put a hat on his head. "Now the hospital." She opened the car door before him and closed it behind him. "Now the emergency room." She left the house lights on, she left the front door unlocked. After backing out of the garage, she didn't close the garage door. She gunned the car backward, into the street. The car squealed.

NOISES, NOISES. Now Steven has the sound track for his film. From *Yin Yang Jerusalem*, Chapter One: The vacuum cleaner, the stereo, the Waring blender, the TV set, freeway traffic, a truck, a pile driver, a DC-10, the Twentieth Century Limited. But the image?

A handheld camera. Fogel is stationed on the lawn—not the lawn in White Plains, but on an empty plain, on a heath in New Jersey. Film: 7247, set wide open, almost overexposed. Focus: the back of Fogel's head, the convex spot exactly opposite the deep place under his brow, between his eyes. The cameraman begins to walk around Fogel. The camera holds level to show the eyes with which Fogel has seen what he has seen, the ears with which he has heard what he has heard. The camera goes around and around him, from east to west and then to east, over again and over again, the cameraman moving back each time imperceptibly—a millimeter, a micromillimeter—hour after hour, his shadow crossing Fogel's and recrossing it until time spends itself, light is gone, Fogel is gone, Fogel's eyes and ears, Fogel's head, disappear into a speck, into dust. Poof! Finished.

"Frontal," the doctor said. "It won't do much good to operate."

"Would it have done any good six months ago?"

The doctor, Cohen, a new one in the White Plains hospital, skimmed over the report of the doctor from Mount Sinai and glanced at the Mount Sinai brain scan. "No. No good at all."

"He knew. My husband knew. All the time, he knew." Lillian's mouth twisted to one side, as if she were the one who had something wrong with her brain. "I didn't know. The doctor didn't know, but *he* knew." Dr. Cohen remained silent. "Will he have a lot of pain if you don't operate?"

The doctor looked at her, expressionless.

"Then operate."

"It's risky, but it's his only chance anyway." The doctor smiled. "If we hit him with some radiation too, there's some chance—" He stopped smiling. "Some chance that he could survive for a while."

Lillian, I will tell you the truth: They cover up for each other. If it would have made no difference six months ago, why is Dr. Cohen hurrying to operate now before Steven can fly in from California? Before Marlene is strong enough to drive in from Boston, although she'll come anyway once she learns what's happening. Why is Dr. Cohen ordering them to push the anesthesia needle into Fogel so soon? Why is Fogel lying on the stretcher? Why is he being wheeled into the elevator at six o'clock in the morning?

Two nurses, both named Marie, worked prepping Fogel. Fogel was asleep. One Marie was swathing his face with bandages, leaving a space beneath his nose so he could breathe. The other Marie was shaving the top of Fogel's head. Before she began shaving, she bent down and kissed it.

Bandage-Marie saw her kissing Fogel. She laughed. "Can't leave the boys alone!" she said.

Razor-Marie giggled. "I always do it." She was a plump nurse with a nasal voice. "Even with women. Just to wish them luck." Suddenly Razor-Marie was all business. She set to work with her scissors energetically, cutting Fogel's hair like an angry barber.

"Don't think I'm not watching you." Bandage-Marie slipped her hands under Fogel's head. She grasped Fogel's head and held it up. "You kiss the boys harder."

Razor-Marie switched on the electric razor and went over Fogel's scalp, neatening the territory she had shorn.

As soon as she had finished, Bandage-Marie reached for her bandage-roll and her scissors. She picked up Fogel's head again and began wrapping bandages around it. Then she moved sideways, stepping out of Razor-Marie's way. Razor-Marie started lathering Fogel's scalp with shaving cream from an aerosol can. Then she smoothed it with a plastic hand razor.

Razor-Marie set the razor down. Fogel took a deep, unconscious breath. He exhaled. While he was inhaling and exhaling, both Maries kept still, watching him. After he began breathing normally again, Bandage-Marie handed the end of the bandage to Razor-Marie. Now Razor-Marie was also Bandage-Marie. She finished covering Fogel's head, leaving an unwrapped space above the frontal lobe where she had shaved. "I won't kiss him again," she said. "Once is enough." Over her heart she made the sign of the cross.

Downstairs in the hospital cafeteria, Lillian was drinking her second cup of coffee. In Boston, Teddy was standing in front of his eight o'clock class, shooting black unemployment statistics at them. Marlene was speeding along the Connecticut Turnpike at sixty miles an hour, heading toward the hospital. In her hand she clutched a quarter for the exact-change lane so she wouldn't lose any time if a toll booth came up soon.

Dr. Cohen made a coronal incision approximately four inches long across the bald place on Fogel's skull. "Am I going to be bald like Grandpa?" Steven had once asked when he was eight years old, riding back to White Plains after a visit to the Bronx to see Lillian's father. "Don't ask such questions!" Lillian had said. Grandpa had been wheezing through much of the visit. "We never know what the fates have in store for us," Fogel had answered. Now Fogel was as bald as Grandpa. Dr. Cohen peeled Fogel's scalp skin back. The attending resident, a tall, skinny Yale graduate, clamped it. Then the sawing started.

Dr. Cohen always did his own sawing. When the sawing began, the resident started to hold his breath. Dr. Cohen was no Giotto, he didn't produce a perfect circle. Nevertheless, as soon as Dr. Cohen finished the sawing, the resident said, "A perfect circle!" A nurse, dressed in green, with her face masked, was waiting to receive Fogel's skull-lid. She held it with tongs and set it into a silvery basin resting on a silvery table. The operating-room walls were pale green, the same color as the nurse's smock. The resident leaned over to inspect the skull-lid. "Here!" Dr. Cohen commanded. The resident swiveled his attention back to Fogel's head. There, revealed, was Fogel's brain—pale, pinkish, jelly-white.

Another coronal incision. Dr. Cohen's knuckles turned white with effort as he tried to pierce only the dura mater and nothing else. The skull-lid nurse's eyes shut. "Suction!" Dr. Cohen suddenly commanded. "It's flooding." On

193

"flooding," his voice rose, as if he were a singer not a surgeon. The nurse's eyes opened, her hands whirled, she reached, she inserted. Her assistant switched on: The suction tube sucked. Fogel's blood swished into the tube. Dr. Cohen's cheeks puffed out. He exhaled. "Not arterial," he called out.

"Arachnoid blood lake," the resident whispered.

"Not arachnoid." Dr. Cohen began peeling back the brain-layer he had just cut. He turned to the resident and ordered, "Clamp!"

The resident clamped.

"I think I see it," Dr. Cohen said. "It's not one of those dark bastards."

"Anaplastic," the resident murmured as if he were proposing a hypothesis, not asking a question.

Dr. Cohen began to slice through Fogel's arachnoid membrane; he peeled it back and started feeling around in Fogel's subarachnoid space. This was where Fogel had felt the headaches. This was where the pressure had been, sometimes toward the forehead, now cut in half, sometimes toward the temple, now covered with bandages. Dr. Cohen's fingers probed through veins, pushing them aside. Under the bandages, under the skullbone, resting until they were needed again, were the cells which had moved Fogel's feet onto the train cars traveling from Drohobych to Auschwitz, from Auschwitz to Belsen; the cells which had moved Fogel's tongue to pisslicking on the day when he was forced to be a pisslicker. These cells were still protected, concealed under Fogel's skull. Exposed and visible, pulsing through the pia mater, pink and white in Fogel's frontal lobe, were the cells which had decided: First, that there is no God; and then—Didn't even Voltaire admit it? Didn't Lessing? And neither of them was subject to headaches!—that perhaps God really

194

does exist; and finally—after the aspirins, after the acupuncture, after the psychotherapy, after even the prayers—that, actually, there is no God. There is only—but to what good?—enlightenment. And from enlightenment what comes? CAT scans? National Socialism?

Dr. Cohen cut.

Through the pia mater, through the folds of the cortex, into the white matter. "Anaplastic," Dr. Cohen said. The resident nodded. "Anaplastic," he repeated.

"At least it's not one of those big black bastards!" Dr. Cohen sighed. "It's white."

"Easier." The resident nodded again. "Easier than glioblastoma multiforma."

"Black bastard!" That's what one of the nurses, a small pockmarked woman, had called her husband the previous evening when he'd come home at 11:30 P.M. instead of six. Beneath her mask, she smiled. Then she looked down at Fogel's brain, exposed, white and pink, lying in front of her. It wasn't white and pink any longer. It was turning dark; it was bloody red. "Suction!" Dr. Cohen shouted. "Suction!" The black nurse moved in fast with the suction tube. The resident pushed in close. He clamped off the vein that had been cut. With the fingers of his left hand, Dr. Cohen probed to see where the anaplastic astrocytoma—that was it, an anaplastic astrocytoma—stopped and the frontal lobe of Fogel's brain began, where Fogel's anterior cerebral artery began. Dr. Cohen reached down very slowly, using both hands now, the fingers and the knife, very slowly, to separate it, very slowly, to extricate Fogel from it. "Suction! Suction!" he suddenly shouted again. "Suction! Suction!"

In the coffee shop, Lillian was sitting at the counter, talking to a woman from Tuckahoe, an Italian woman whose husband was being catheterized to see if he might need a bypass operation; maybe he'd only need a pacemaker. "Don't worry," Lillian said, "everything will turn out OK." The Italian woman's eyes were the same color as the coffee she was drinking. She put her hand on Lillian's arm. But she didn't say "Don't worry" to Lillian. She didn't say "Everything will be all right." She remained silent.

Lillian waved her hand at the waitress and pointed to a pile of doughnuts sitting on a cake stand in front of her. The waitress handed her a plump jelly doughnut on a paper plate. Lillian picked it up and took a large bite. Powdered sugar spilled on her dress, jelly smeared her chin. She didn't reach for a napkin. "My daughter should be here by now," she said. "My poor daughter."

"Where is she coming from?"

Lillian told the Italian woman about her daughter. She told her about her son-in-law and about her late grandson.

Again the woman put her hand on Lillian's arm. "God is testing you," she said.

Lillian pressed her finger against the doughnut. "If this is a test—" She shook her head from side to side. "If this is a test, I flunk."

At Star of David Cemetery, Farmingdale, Long Island, Steven steps forward. At last 1489A is being filled. The coffin contains the bruised head, the cut brow, everything that's left of the late Chaim Fogel of White Plains, for many years associate professor of history at New York University, beloved husband of Lillian, dear father of Steven of Los Angeles and Marlene Jessep of Boston. Steven shivers. It's much colder here than on the Coast, April but still winter. The operation was a failure, though nothing had metastasized. Primary brain tumors do not metastasize. They just grow.

196

"Magnified and sanctified be the Great Name of the Lord." As befits a son at his father's funeral, Steven recites words of praise before God. He finds it difficult to pronounce some of the words of praise. How many years has it been since Steven has read Hebrew? Even longer than it's been since he's worn a necktie. (Now he's wearing a blue-and-silver tie, rich-looking but sober, borrowed from the wardrobe of the deceased.) Steven's been exposed, almost overexposed, you might say, to his father's enlightened teachings. Nevertheless, he reads the prayer in a loud, dramatic voice, vigorously calling out each holy word: Magnified, sanctified, blessed, honored, exalted, praised, raised up, set on high, elevated be God's name. Now, calling out these words, only now is Steven a Jew.

But how can Steven make a Jewish film without the star? This makes Steven cry. Now all he has for the film is the sound track. The image of Fogel standing alone on an empty plain is gone. Nothing is left of Fogel, nothing but his name.

No image.

No image?

Perhaps the bread of affliction, an image which Fogel himself once suggested for such a film? Or better still names, merely names—Chaim Fogel, Hannah Kalb, Pittel Gewirtz—all of them dead, no longer survivors, each one alone on a page in the Book of Life, surrounded by space filled with deeds which only God can see.

"The name of the film is *GOD,*" Steven said to Rochelle.

Providentially, Rochelle had been promoted to a new job at the Holocaust Memorial—public relations liaison person. Now she was the one Steven had to talk to about getting backing for his film proposal. It was clear that Rochelle wanted to get married. "We have a lot in common," she had said when she and Steven had first met at the Holocaust Memorial. "Auschwitz. Both my parents." But Rochelle was older than Steven.

"GOD," Steven said again, giving the word a little French twist as if he were already at Cannes. The previous evening he had taken Rochelle out to a retrospective—two works by Jean Renoir. Now Rochelle was having a planning session with him in her office. She was sitting with her mouth open a little, as if she were an actress in a TV commercial. But Rochelle wasn't smiling.

"If you use that name for it, that's breaking the second commandment," she said. She thought about that for a moment. "No, maybe it's breaking the third."

"There won't be any pictures of God."

"Not the graven images commandment. The commandment against taking the name in vain." Now Rochelle smiled, but solemnly.

"This isn't in vain!" Round-hipped, round-breasted, but stupid. Still, in control of the money. "I thought of an alternate title: *Who Shall Die.*"

That title was too negative for Rochelle, too negative even for the Holocaust Memorial.

"How about *G-D*?"

"That's unusual." Rochelle looked relieved. "It's provocative too. I'll see if I can clear it with the board."

Un film: *G-D,* or *Who Shall Die.*

Produced with the assistance of a grant from the Holocaust Memorial Foundation, Los Angeles, California.

Cinéaste: Steven Fogel. Réalisateur: Steven Fogel. Caméra: Steven Fogel. Avec: Chaim Fogel. Even though Chaim Fogel is dead.

Even though the cinéaste has said, "G-d is a shit!" Even

though he has said, "How could G-d pull a number like the Holocaust on the Jews? How could G-d run that kind of act on my father?"

Foolish boy! I tell you, I run whatever act I choose to run. I am The Author. I am The Réalisateur. I am The Cinéaste.

Is it not written: The Lord has done that which He has devised?

Is it not written: He hath fulfilled His word which He had commanded in the days of old?

Is it not written: Behold I, even I, am against thee and will execute judgments in the midst of thee in the sight of the nations?

Is it not written: The Lord was an enemy?

Is it not written: He hath thrown down and hath not pitied?

Foolish boy! Do you think that only Fogel is made in My image? Isn't Hitler made in My image too?

But to you "The gates of perception are closed." Source: Maimonides, *Guide for the Perplexed*, XXXI. For, as it is written: Thou canst not see My Face, for there no man shall see Me and live.

Foolish boy! I do not discuss theology with Jews. I only give commandments. You decide whether or not to fulfill them. For as it is written: Everything is foreseen, yet freedom of choice is given.

Foolish Jew! Should I have left Chaim Fogel among the unborn? Should I have created him as one of the animals, or given him life as a leaf or a color or a sound? No, I made him a Jew. As it is written: I have made all My goodness pass before thee and I will be gracious to whom I am gracious and will show mercy on whom I shall show mercy.

I delivered him from the house of slavery.

I rescued him from the sword.

I prepared banquets before him.

I avenged him of his enemies.

I led him beside still waters. I gave him a virtuous woman, her price above rubies.

I gave his children a place of refuge.

I gave him Meissen china, graduate students, bibliographies, silk neckties, Terry: many delights.

Foolish Jew! You make films and think you finish them, but you don't know how they end. Only I say "finished." Only I know the outcome. For you and your son and your grandson. For your sister's son, Chaim Garrison Jessep. For his son and his grandson. For as it is written: Yet will I leave a remnant.

Praise Me.